P. A. Stuart

The Inside Guide To
Android Tablets
For Seniors

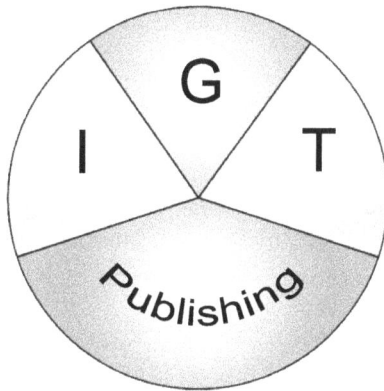

1st Edition

Covers Android KitKat & Jelly Bean

The Inside Guide to
Android Tablets For Seniors

Published by IGT Publishing

ISBN-13: 978-0993266188
ISBN-10: 0993266185

Contents

Chapter 5 – Your Tablet's Software

Chapter 6 – Getting Connected

Chapter 7 – Using The Internet

Chapter 8 – Staying in Touch

Chapter 9 – Organizing Your Life

Chapter 10 – Recreation

Chapter 11 – Reading

Chapter 12 – Google Now

Chapter 13 – Security

Chapter 14 – Third-Party Apps

Chapter 15 – Troubleshooting & Maintenance

Index

CHAPTER 1

Introduction to Android Tablets

Currently all the rage, tablets are incredibly useful devices that offer something to all age groups. The tablet market is dominated by two types – the iPad that runs Apple's iOS operating system, and Android tablets that run Google's Android operating system. The latter are made by a number of manufacturers and are the ones we will be looking at in this book.

In Chapter One, we take a look at the models available from the various manufacturers and see what each type has to offer. We also take a general look at the Android operating system and explain its pro's and con's.

For the older generation, who struggle to understand much of the computer-speak and jargon associated with computing, we take time out to explain some of the terminology they will encounter with regard to tablets.

Introduction

In this book, we are using Google's Nexus tablet to demonstrate how tablets, Android, and apps work. Please note, however, that there are many different manufacturers of Android tablets and so there may be minor discrepancies between your tablet and what's in the book.

The same applies to Android itself. While the version of Android we describe here is the 'pure' or 'unadulterated' version as supplied by Google, if your tablet is not a Nexus, you may find that the version on it is not quite the same. This is because manufacturers of Android devices are allowed to modify Android, and do.

Also, your device may provide an app store other than Google's Play Store; your manufacturer may have replaced some of the default Google apps with different versions; and some of the settings screens we describe may be different.

All that said, any differences you encounter will be minor, and will not make the explanations and how-to steps in the book any less clear.

What is a Tablet?

Tablets are portable, or mobile, computers. They consist of a self-contained unit that includes a touchscreen display, internal circuitry, a battery, and switches for power and volume control. Virtually all tablets also offer a camera (some have two), a microphone, a loudspeaker, and ports for connecting to a computer and battery charging.

They are light and very thin, with the mini versions being small enough to fit into a large pocket. This is largely due to the fact that tablets do not need a physical keyboard (although these can be attached if desired). Instead, they use what's known as a 'virtual keyboard' that automatically appears on the touchscreen whenever a text field is opened. To enter text, you just tap on the required key.

Similarly, navigating around a tablet, opening and closing apps, etc, is done by tapping on virtual buttons and by using finger gestures, such as tapping and swiping.

Tablets are not suitable for the resource-hungry applications that run on computers, and so are not a substitute for them. However, low-resource applications, such as email, the Internet, playing music, etc, run perfectly well on tablets.

Essentially then, a tablet is a cross between a computer and a smartphone; less capable than the former and more capable than the latter.

Tablet Classification

Tablets are classified in a number of categories and subcategories depending on factors such as whether or not they provide a physical keyboard and the method of accessing the screen. These can be boiled down to the following:

- Slates

- Hybrids

- Convertibles

Lets look at these in more detail:

Slates

Slates do not have a physical keyboard and so require the use of a virtual keyboard. They are not supplied with a protective cover and have no moving parts.

For these reasons, these are the smallest and lightest of the various types of tablet. Examples of Slate tablets are the iPad and the Nexus

Hybrids

A Hybrid tablet consists of two separate halves – the top half is the tablet with a built-in screen and the bottom half is a physical keyboard that snaps into place. In operation, they are much like a small laptop.

The keyboard base usually provides extra ports and connections, such as USB. Microsoft's Surface that runs Windows 8 is a typical example of a Hybrid tablet.

Convertibles

Convertibles can be used as either a laptop or a tablet. In laptop mode, the screen sits at approximately ninety degrees to the keyboard, while in tablet mode, it swivels right and lies flush with the back of the keyboard, which is thus hidden.

Convertible tablets provide a virtual keyboard as the physical keyboard is inaccessible when in tablet mode.

What Can You Do With a Tablet?

Tablets offer significant advantages over computers in certain respects. The main reason for this is that they run streamlined operating systems that result in them having much lower power requirements. This provides a number of benefits such as mobility and near-instant on/off switching.

In terms of what you can actually do with them, the following are the most common uses for these devices:

- **Browsing the Internet** – from the comfort of your favorite armchair, you can book holidays, buy just about any product known to man, get information on any subject, and engage in social networking such as Facebook and Twitter

- **Communication** – tablets let you send & receive email, text messages, make video calls and, in the case of cellular models, make and receive phone calls

- **Music** – listening to music is a very popular use of tablets. You can upload your own music collection to the device and/or buy music from Google's Play Store

- **Photography** – virtually all tablets provide a camera (although the quality of these can vary considerably) with which to take pictures and home videos. You can also upload your photo collection to your tablet both for your own viewing and for showing to others

- **Reading** – due to their dimensions, tablets are ideal for reading the written word. You can quickly build up a book library by buying ebooks from the Play Store. If you have a Kindle account, you can install the Kindle app and access all your Kindle books on the device

- **Movies and TV** – just as with music and books, a huge range of movies and TV programs are available. Having downloaded them to your tablet, you can then watch them wherever you happen to be

- **Games** – literally thousands of games across all genres are available for download to your tablet – some free, some not

- **Business** – the Google Play Store is packed with apps that let you take notes, plan meetings, and write, edit and scan documents; all on a slim, portable device that you can carry with you while commuting, attending meetings, etc

- **Navigation** – tablets are great devices for finding your way around. Google Earth and Google Maps are default apps on most Android tablets, plus you can download more from the Play Store

Manufacturers & Models

Unlike Apple's iOS and Microsoft's Windows operating systems, the Android operating system is open-source, which means it can be used by anyone. In an attempt to compete with Apple's iPad and Microsoft's Surface tablets, a number of manufacturers have built tablets around Android.

Some typical examples are:

Nexus 7

Manufactured by ASUS and running Android Jelly Bean 4.3, the Nexus is a premium quality tablet in all respects.

The 7-inch tablet has a storage capacity of up to 32 GB and a screen resolution of 1200 x 1920, with a pixel density of 323 ppi.

The processor is a quad-core 1.5GHz Qualcomm Snapdragon S4 Pro that provides very good performance.

With regard to networking, the Nexus features the 802.11 a/b/g/n dual-band Wi-Fi standard, Bluetooth 4.0 and NFC.

As a result, browsing the Internet with the Nexus 7 is impressively fast. Web pages open almost instantaneously and large apps download very quickly.

Lenova IdeaTab

This lower quality tablet is made by Lenovo and runs Android Ice Cream Sandwich 4.0. A 7-inch device, the IdeaTab is solidly constructed and comes with a 1 GHz Cortex-A9 processor and 1 GB of memory.

The display is a 600 x 1024 pixels screen with a pixel density of 170 ppi. While adequate, it has to be said that this screen is not the tablet's strongest feature.

Other features include 802.11 b/g/n Wi-Fi, Bluetooth 3.0, and Accelerometer and Proximity sensors.

Storage is 32 GB and there is a microSD card slot provided should more be needed. In common with most tablets. the IdeaTab provides two cameras – a 3.15 megapixel main camera and a lower quality VGA camera.

Venue 7

Made by Dell, the Venue 7 is a stylish and well made Android tablet. It features a durable and very attractive aluminum body and an extremely thin bezel.

The high-definition 7-inch IPS screen provides a resolution of 1200 × 800 pixels, and an unusually wide viewing angle.

Featuring a dual-core 1.6 GHz Intel Z3460 Atom processor together with 1 GB of memory, the tablet is a snappy performer.

The Venue comes with two cameras – a rear-facing 5 MP main camera and a lower quality 1 MP front-facing camera.

The tablet runs Android KitKat 4.4.2.

Xperia Z2

Manufactured by Sony, the Xperia Z2 is one of the thinnest and lightest tablets on the market. It is available in 8 inch and 10 inch versions. An unusual feature is that the tablet is waterproof; something that not even the iPads offer.

The display is a high-definition IPS screen with a resolution of 1920 x 1200. A feature of IPS screens is the excellent viewing angles and the Z2 is no exception in this respect.

Inside the tablet is a 2.226 GHz Qualcomm Snapdragon 801 quad-core processor which, together with the 3 GB of memory, result in a very smooth performance.

With regard to storage, there are 16 and 32 GB models available. The tablet also offers a microSD card slot that makes it possible to add up to 128 GB. Connectivity is provided by 802.1ac Wi-Fi, NFC and Bluetooth 4.0.

The Z3 is supplied with Android KitKat 4.4.2.

Galaxy Tab 3

This tablet comes from the South Korean electronics giant, Samsung. Weighing in at just 300 grams, the tablet is not only lightweight but also extremely slim, at just 6.6 mm.

The Galaxy Tab 3 has a 7-inch screen and, while the viewing angles are good thanks to IPS, the 1024 x 600 resolution is somewhat average.

Inside the case is a dual-core 1.2 GHz Marvell Armada PXA986 processor and 1 GB of memory. Storage capacity is 8 or 16 GB, which can be expanded by up 32 GB via a microSD card slot.

Included with the tablet is a single 3.2 MP camera that takes pictures of average quality. With regard to network connectivity, the Galaxy Tab S offers 802.11a/b/g/n Wi-Fi, HSPA, LTE, Bluetooth, and a microUSB 2.0 port.

The tablet runs Android Jelly Bean 4.1.

Fire HD 6

Somewhat lower in overall quality than most of the other tablets on the market, Amazon's Fire HD 6 tablet does have one big advantage – it's a lot more affordable.

While the thick, plain bezel is unattractive, it nevertheless houses a respectable 1.5 GHz MediaTek quad-core processor, 1 GB of memory and either 8 or 16 GB's of internal storage space. Note that there is no microSD slot with which to add more.

The tablet has an IPS 6-inch screen with a 1280 x 800, 252 ppi, high-definition resolution that provides a picture quality that is surprisingly good given the price.

Networking is provided by 802.11b/g/n Wi-Fi.

With regard to taking pictures, the Fire HD is supplied with a 2 MP rear camera that can only be described as average, and a front-facing VGA camera.

The operating system is Amazon's Android-based Fire OS 4 Sangria.

Galaxy Note 10.1

Another tablet from the Samsung stable, the Galaxy Note with its 10.1 inch screen is thin, light and easy to handle. It comes with its own Bluetooth keyboard, which can also act as a cover.

Attractively styled, the Note Pro has some impressive specifications. These include a custom 1.9 GHz quad-core Exynos processor, 3 GB of memory, 32 or 64 GB's of internal storage, an 8 megapixel rear camera and Samsung's integrated S Pen stylus.

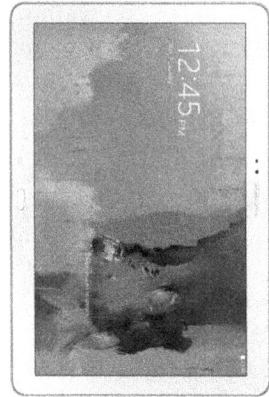

The latter is a rubber-tipped plastic stylus that allows you to draw or write on the tablet's display, making it possible to use various applications linked to naturalistic handwriting and pin-point navigation.

Connectivity and networking is provided by Wi-Fi, Bluetooth 4.0, a microUSB 3.0 port with microUSB 2.0 compatibility, NFC, and GPS.

The tablet is supplied with Android KitKat 4.4.2.

Yoga Tablet 2

From the Chinese manufacturer, Lenovo, the Yoga Tablet 2 is available in 8.4 and 10 inch versions. An unusual feature not found with other tablets is the built-in kickstand that lets you prop up the device at any desired angle.

Positioned in the middle of the tablet market, the Yoga 2 features a 1920 x 1200 IPS display, 2 GB of memory, and Intel's Atom Z3745 processor.

Storage capacity is a relatively low 16 GB but this can be expanded to 64 GB via the microSD slot; something you won't find on the much more expensive iPads.

The tablet comes with an 8 megapixel camera that takes pictures of just average quality – definitely not one of its best features. This accolade must go to its amazing battery life, which can be up to 18 hours.

The Yoga 2 is supplied with Android KitKat 4.4.2.

Android in a Nutshell

Android tablets are so named after the operating system on which they run. In order to get the best out of your tablet, it is important you have some understanding of Android.

What is Android?

Android is an operating system designed for use with mobile devices such as smartphones and tablet computers. It provides a platform that links all the various elements of the electronic devices that use it, and the applications, or apps, that run on these devices. It has the same function as Apple's iOS, and Microsoft's Windows, operating systems.

Devices that run Android use touch inputs that loosely correspond to real-world actions, like swiping, tapping, pinching, and reverse pinching to manipulate on-screen objects, and a virtual keyboard.

Android's source code is released by Google under open source licenses, although most Android devices ultimately ship with a combination of open source and proprietary software. Android is popular with technology companies, who require a ready-made, low-cost and customizable operating system for high-tech devices.

Because basically anyone can use it, a large community of Android developers has built up. This in turn has resulted in versions of Android being available for a range of devices, such as game consoles, digital cameras, desktop computers, and other electronic devices.

As of February 2014, there were in excess of one and a quarter million Android apps in Google's Play Store, while the majority of smartphones and tablets use the Android operating system.

Updating Android

Because so many manufacturers have created their own versions of Android, and on a range of different products, Android updates have to be individually tailored for each separate device. This is in contrast to Apple and Windows devices, where just one update version is required.

As a result, delays in rolling out the various updates are common and, typically, it can be anywhere between six and nine months before a device receives an update. The exception to this are Nexus tablets, which are Google's own brand, and so are the first to be updated.

Google provides major incremental upgrades to Android every six to nine months, with confectionery-themed names. The latest major release is Android KitKat and is the one featured in this book along with its predecessor, Android Jelly Bean – the two are very similar.

The Android/Google Connection

While operating systems such as Android, iOS and Windows 8, and the apps that run on these systems, are an integral part of mobile computing, there is another aspect that is becoming increasingly important – namely online services, which can only be accessed via a registered account.

For example, both Apple with its iOS operating system and apps, and Microsoft with its Windows 8 equivalents, allow registered users to access online stores from which they can buy and download apps.

Then there is Android, which is of course synonymous with Google. Buy an Android tablet and you are automatically enrolled into the Google ecosystem, like it or not – the Android/Google connection.

One of the first actions you will take when setting up your new Android tablet is to either sign in to an existing Google account, or create one. Having done so, you will then be able to access and use the following Google services:

- **Online stores** – for example, the Play Store for downloading apps

- **Google Calendar** – this displays a list of all Google calendar events

- **Google Drive** – this allows you to save and view data online

- **Gmail** – access your Google email account online or on any device

- **Google Keep** – create and organize notes, lists and photos online

- **Google Maps** – find local businesses, view maps and get directions

The above are just some of the online services offered by Google. Note that these services are all synchronized across your Android devices. For example, if you read and then delete an email on your smartphone, it will be automatically deleted on your tablet. Create a note on your tablet and you will be able to edit or delete the same note on your smartphone.

Other benefits of a Google account include:

- Access to your account from any mobile device or computer at **accounts.google.com**. Here, you will find numerous options such as configuring your security settings, editing your personal information, changing your password, and much more

- Your account, settings and data will be automatically backed up to Google's servers

Tablet Terminology

Before we dive in to Android tablets and see what they do and how, it may be helpful to offer a brief explanation of some of the terminology you are going to encounter in this book. Note that some of these terms are not restricted to tablets.

3G and 4G

3G and 4G are voice and data networks that mobile devices use to make calls and connect to the Internet. Access usually requires a usage agreement with a mobile service provider. While 4G provides faster connection speeds than 3G, both are slightly slower than Wi-Fi and can prove unreliable outside densely populated areas.

App

Short for application, an app is a computer program designed to run on mobile devices such as smartphones and tablet computers. Apps are available from online stores which, typically, are operated by device manufacturers such as Apple, Google, Microsoft and Blackberry. Some apps are free, while others must be paid for.

Aspect Ratio

Aspect ratio is the relationship between screen height and width. To fill a tablet screen with movies and other wide-screen content, an aspect ratio of 16:9 is ideal. Tablets allow the user to easily switch between Landscape (wide) mode and Portrait (tall) mode.

Bluetooth

Bluetooth is a short-range wireless technology that transmits data between two devices. It is generally used to connect peripherals such as mice, keyboards and headsets to computers or mobile devices. It is built into millions of consumer products.

Cloud Computing

Cloud computing is a term that refers to the storage (and accessing) of data and programs over the Internet, rather than on a computing device. The word 'cloud' is just a metaphor for the Internet. Cloud computing can also refer to off-site backup of data. In this case, data on a computing device is synchronized with a remote server. If the data is subsequently erased from the device, or changed, the device can resynchronize with the remote server and thus reload the deleted or original data.

GB

GB is a commonly used acronym that stands for gigabyte and refers to the memory or storage capacity of a tablet or other device.

Touchscreen
A touchscreen is a type of screen used with smartphones and tablets that allows the user to control the device by tapping, swiping, pinching or reverse-pinching it.

Operating System
An operating system is the software responsible for controlling a tablet, computer or smartphone's hardware. Examples of tablet operating systems include Android, iOS and Windows 8.

Processor
A processor is effectively the brain of a computing device. Its power, or speed, is measured in gigahertz, e,g 2 GHz. The higher the number, the faster it operates. Some devices have quad-core processors, while most use dual- or single-core processors. A quad-core processor can run four simultaneous processes and so be extremely quick, but it will also use up battery power at a correspondingly rapid rate.

Resolution and PPI
Resolution dictates how sharp the screen is as a measure of the pixels. Full high-definition (HD) is 1920 x 1080 pixels, but screen size is a factor as well, so you'll often see PPI (pixels per inch, e.g. 266 ppi). The higher it is, the sharper the screen.

Sensor
A sensor is an electronic device that responds to its environment and produces an electric current that alters in relation to a specific change in that environment. Sensors play an important role in mobile devices, giving them much of their functionality. Commonly used sensors in tablets include ambient light, GPS, compass, proximity and pressure sensors, plus gyroscopes and accelerometers.

Synchronization
Synchronization is a technique that maintains and updates sets of data on two or more devices by automatically copying changes back and forth. For example, a user's contact list on one device can be synchronized with other devices or computers. Data synchronization can be 'local' where the device and computer are side-by-side, or 'remote' where the user is mobile and the data is synchronized over a mobile network.

Wi-Fi
Wi-Fi (short for Wireless Fidelity) is a wireless network technology that enables mobile devices such as tablets and smartphones to connect to the Internet via a wireless network access point, or hotspot. In the home, these access points are provided by wireless routers that are part of the home owner's broadband setup. Wi-Fi is usually free to use.

What to Look For in a Tablet

There is a huge range of tablets from which to choose and unless you know what to look for, you will quite probably end up with something that is either unsuitable for your requirements, costs more than you need have paid, or maybe even both. So when in the market for a new tablet, the factors you should consider are:

- Operating System
- Manufacturer
- Apps
- Features
- Price

Operating System

As we have already seen, a tablet's operating system is a program that manages the device's hardware and software resources, and provides common services for the apps that run on it.

Currently, there are three main choices: Apple's iOS, Microsoft's Windows 8, and Google's Android. In terms of functionality and reliability, there is little to choose between them. However, the 'walled garden' approach taken by Apple does mean that iOS is, by far, the most secure.

Another issue to consider is that of updates. Updates from Apple and Microsoft are delivered immediately; Android updates can take several months – some device manufacturers take much longer than others.

Also important, particularly to seniors, is how easy the operating system is to learn. Apple's iOS has the advantage here, being simple, more intuitive, and thus easier to get to grips with than Windows 8 and Android – Windows 8, in particular, involves quite a steep learning curve.

Manufacturer

With Apple, the issue is simple – absolutely everything is in-house. Buy an Apple tablet and you know just who you are dealing with in all aspects. This is in contrast to Google and Microsoft who license their operating systems to other tablet manufacturers.

Apple have built a reputation based on high quality and service that can be taken for granted This is not always the case with the manufacturers of Android and Windows tablets though. While there are many excellent tablets from both, you do need to take more care by checking who manufactures the device, their returns policy, service level, and so on.

Apps

Apple, Google and Microsoft keep their apps in the App Store, Play Store and Windows Store respectively.

Currently, the App Store has in the region of 1.2 million apps, the Play Store has 1.4 million, and the Windows Store has .2 million. Clearly, Apple and Google have the advantage here.

It's not just about quantity though – quality is a more important factor and, in this respect, Apple and Google are about the same. The quality of Microsoft's Windows 8 apps, however, are generally much poorer.

Features
Features you must consider include the screen, connectivity, storage capacity, camera, and performance:

- Tablets, typically, are available with a screen size of either 7 or 10 inches. The former is sufficient for reading ebooks, social networking, etc. Watching movies, playing games, and browsing the Internet will be better served with a 10 inch screen. You should also consider the screen's resolution as this determines its clarity

- All tablets come with Wi-Fi with which to access the Internet, send and receive email, send text messages, etc. However, you may want permanent access, in which case you will have to pay the premium for a 3G or 4G enabled tablet, i.e. a cellular model

- A tablet's storage capacity is the amount of data it can hold. Currently, tablets are being sold with capacities between 4 GB and 64 GB. Many also provide a microSD card option with which to expand their capacity

   This should only be an issue if you plan to use your tablet to store large amounts of multimedia, such as home videos, movies, and pictures. As a guide, a two hour movie will use approximately 3.6 GB of storage

- If you engage in social media, a tablet that offers a camera is a must. Some offer two – a main camera and a second lower-quality one for social media. The quality of these cameras can vary considerably and is indicated by their megapixel resolution

- With regard to performance, the thing to consider is the tablet's processor, or CPU. Single-core processors support basic tasks such as browsing the web, email and playing simple games. Dual- and quad-core CPUs take a tablet's performance to a much higher level

Price
Apple's iPads are considered to be the best on the market. However, they are also the most expensive and may well provide a level of quality and features that you don't need. This is why Android tablets appeal to so many people – you should be able to find one that meets all your requirements without having to pay a premium.

CHAPTER 2

The Basics of an Android Tablet

In Chapter Two, we get more specific. We take a look at a typical example of an Android tablet using Google's Nexus as an example, and see the physical controls provided with the tablet. We also see how to keep the tablet's battery charged up and the procedure for connecting it to a computer. The latter can be useful for transferring data such as pictures and video to and from the tablet.

The Home screen is a major part of any tablet and you will learn how to use it to access the tablet's apps, settings and other functions.

We finish with a look at Android's Notifications feature, which keeps you updated with events as they happen; and Quick Settings, which lets you access and configure commonly used settings.

Physical Controls

All tablets are mostly controlled by finger gestures on the touchscreen. However, they all also have some physical controls and, while these may vary between models, they are very similar in function. Below, we see the controls for the Nexus:

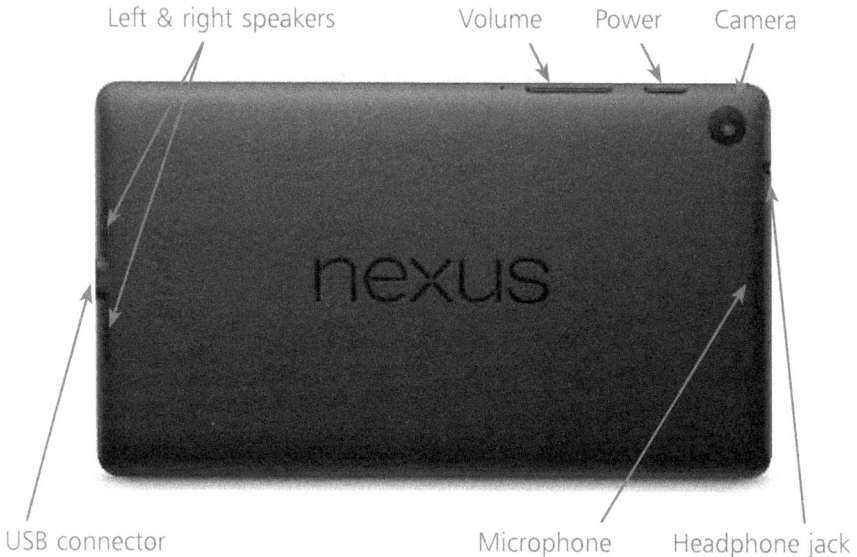

Left & right speakers   Volume   Power   Camera

USB connector   Microphone   Headphone jack

Power Button – press and hold for two seconds to switch the tablet on or off. Press once to put the tablet to sleep or to wake it up

Volume Button – press the top half of the rocker switch to increase the volume and the lower half to decrease it

Headphone Jack – if you want to use a headset with your tablet, this is the place to connect it

USB Socket – your tablet is supplied with a USB cable with which to charge the battery or to connect it to a computer. Plug the cable's small connector into this socket

Loudspeakers – situated on either side of the USB connector are the left and right speakers. Note that you will only get stereo when the tablet is held in Portrait mode

Microphone – the microphone is situated at the top-rear of the tablet

Camera – at the top-right of the tablet is the camera lens

Recharging the Battery

All tablets are powered by a built-in Li-ion battery. As a general rule, this type of battery provides approximately 10 hours of normal use. Heavy duty applications will, however, run it down more quickly.

When the time comes to recharge your device, you have two ways to go: The first is to connect the tablet to the power supply with the supplied USB adapter. This plugs into the power socket and you then plug the USB connector into this. The other end of the cable connects to the tablet.

1. Plug the USB cable into the tablet's USB socket

2. Plug the other end of the cable into the adapter

3. Plug the adapter into a power socket. The battery will now start charging and will continue to do so until fully charged

The second way is to connect the USB plug to a USB port on a computer or laptop as we demonstrate on page 24. However, charging the battery this way will take longer than doing it with the adapter.

Note that whichever method you choose, you can still use the tablet while it is being charged.

Connecting a Tablet to a Computer

There are two reasons you may want to connect your tablet to a computer:

- To charge the tablet

- To access its internal storage in order to copy data to or from it

The procedure is as follows:

1. Connect the large end of the USB cable to a USB port on the computer or laptop. Most computers will have one on the front panel; if not though, you will find one at the rear of the computer

2. Connect the other end of the cable to the tablet as shown on page 23

If all you want to do is charge the tablet you need do nothing else – charging will start automatically and continue until the battery is fully charged. If you want to copy data to or from the tablet, do the following:

1. On the computer's keyboard, locate the Windows key (we're assuming here that it is a Windows computer). The key will be on the bottom row next to the Ctrl key. Press the Windows key and the E key simultaneously

2. The 'This PC' or 'My Computer' window will open as shown below:

3. Under 'Devices and drives' you will see your tablet listed (Nexus 7 in our example above). Click on it to open the tablet's internal storage

The Home Screen

Now that you are familiar with the hardware side of your tablet, it's time to look at its software – the Android operating system. When you turn on your tablet for the first time, you are presented with a setup wizard – see pages 30-31 for how to complete it. When you are done, come back to this page.

The first thing you will see having completed the setup wizard is the Home screen. It is comprised of several elements as we see below:

Notifications Bar

Home screen. Your apps and widgets will be located here

Google search box

Favorites Bar. This part of the screen is reserved for the apps you use the most

Navigation Bar   All Apps button

Note that depending on which tablet you have, these elements may be arranged slightly differently. The Home screen's background will probably also be different.

Getting Around Your Tablet

To move around in Android and access its various features, you tap on electronic, or 'virtual', buttons – these pop up as needed. Everything starts from the Home screen though and this screen provides three buttons that will always be available no matter where you are in Android.

These are located at the bottom of the screen as we see below:

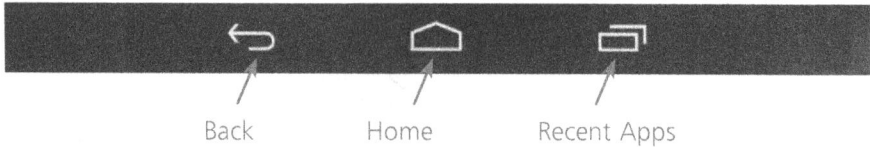

Back   Home   Recent Apps

Back Button – at the left is the Back button. Tap this to return to the previous page or screen

Home Button – the Home button returns you to the most recently viewed home screen

Recent Apps – tapping this button opens a list of recently used apps. Just tap on one of the apps to open it

Another method of going backwards and forwards is swiping – swipe right to go to the next page or screen and swipe left to go to the previous one. A good example of when this is useful is viewing a photo album.

When you are viewing a long page that disappears at the bottom of the screen, you can bring it into view by swiping upwards.

You will find navigation buttons and other controls in apps as well. These can be Back and Forward, Next and Previous, or Forward and Back arrows. In some apps, Gallery for example, the navigation and other controls disappear after a few seconds to 'unclutter' the screen. You can get them back by tapping once on the screen and remove them by tapping again.

All Apps Button – depending on your tablet and the version of Android it is running, you may have an 'All Apps' button on the Favorites Bar as shown on page 25. If you do, tapping this button will open the Apps screen, which shows all the apps installed on your tablet.

Some tabloto, however, don't have an All Apps button. If this is the case with your tablet, you can access the Apps screen by swiping across to the right of the Home screen.

Notifications

A very useful feature provided by tablets is Notifications. The purpose of this is to update you with regard to events that are taking place on your tablet; for example, incoming emails and calendar events. You can also use the feature to remind yourself about forthcoming events, e.g. a lunch date.

Each notification places an icon at the left of the Notification Bar. To see the notifications, swipe downwards from the top-left of the screen. This opens a list with the most recent notification at the top as shown below:

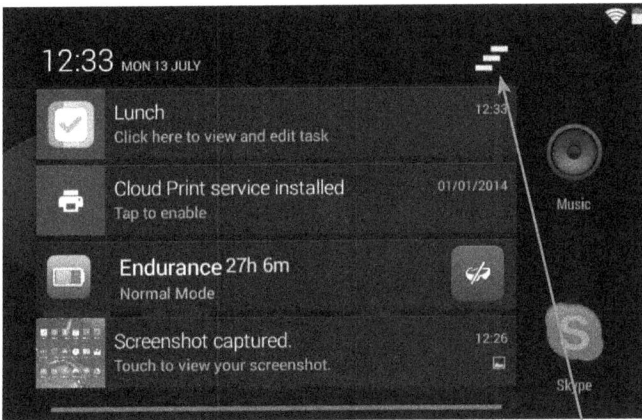

To remove notifications when you have read them, tap this button.

To see more details about a notification, tap on it. It will open in a new screen as we see in the example on the right.

Note that while Android KitKat and Jelly Bean do not provide any settings as such for the Notification feature, it is possible to turn off Notifications on an app-by-app basis.

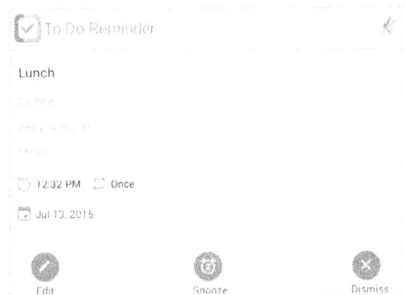

To do this, tap the Home button at the bottom of the screen and then swipe to the left of the screen to open the Apps screen. Tap Settings and then tap Apps.

Tap each app for which you don't want notifications and uncheck the Show notifications checkbox.

Quick Settings

Your tablet has a vast number of settings with which you can configure the device – these are available from the Settings app as we'll see later. Many of the settings, however, will be rarely needed, if at all. Others though, you will use frequently, and this is where Quick Settings comes in handy. To access it, swipe downwards from the top-right of any screen.

At the top of the screen are three icons: the first, Owner, will display a picture of the main account holder (this has to be set up). The second shows the percentage of charge in the battery, and the third opens the main Settings app.

Below at the left is WLAN – this is the Wi-Fi control – tap the icon to turn Wi-Fi on or off. Next to Wi-Fi is Bluetooth. Again, just tap the icon to turn it on or off. At the right of the Bluetooth control is Location. This turns the tablet's Location service on or off. This service tells the tablet its geographical location, information which is used by a number of apps, such as Chrome and Maps.

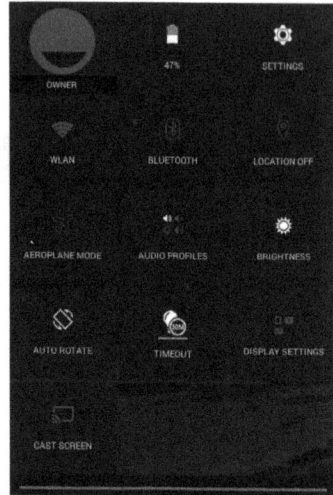

Below these three options are Airplane Mode, Audio Profiles and Brightness. When on, Airplane Mode disables the wireless features of the tablet in order to comply with airline regulations. Audio Profiles gives you a choice of four sound setups – General, Silent, Meeting and Outdoor. If you need to, you can choose one to apply sound settings that suit your current situation. For example, Silent, silences the tablet completely. We'll look at Sound profiles in more detail later. Tap Brightness to open a slider with which you can adjust the tablet's level of brightness.

Moving further down, we have Auto Rotate. This lets you lock the tablet in either Portrait or Landscape mode or let it move between the two as you rotate the tablet. Next is Timeout – this is a power saving feature that lets you specify a period after which the tablet is put to Sleep, i.e. the screen is powered down. The default setting is 15 seconds but you can change this to one minute, two minutes, five minutes, 10 minutes and 30 minutes by tapping repeatedly on the icon. At the right of Timeout is Display Settings, which lets you make changes to the display's settings.

Finally, at the bottom, there is an option called Cast screen. This lets you mirror your tablet's screen on a TV and can be a great way to share your photos or watch a video on a big screen. It requires the use of Chromecast – a media streaming device that plugs into your TV's HDMI port.

CHAPTER 3

Setting Up Your Tablet

When you first switch on your tablet, you are presented with a setup wizard that walks you through a series of important configuration settings. We explain what these settings are so that you make the right choices.

That's just the beginning though – there are a huge number of other settings that, amongst other things, let you personalize your tablet in terms of sound and visuals such as the background image, user accounts, security, language and many more.

All these settings are available from the Settings app.

Setup Wizard

When your tablet is switched on for the first time, you will be presented with a setup wizard. This runs you through the major configuration settings; the minor ones can be done later.

The settings configured by the wizard are as follows:

1. **Language, Region & Time Zone** – the opening setting provides you with two options: select your language and select your time zone. You should find that these are correctly selected by default

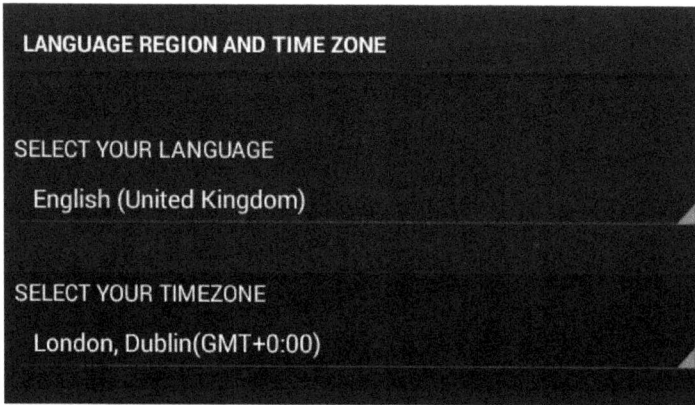

2. **License Agreement** – you are asked to OK the license agreement – tap ACCEPT

3. **Wi-Fi Network** – to setup a Wi-Fi connection, tap SCAN. You will now see a list of all the Wi-Fi networks within range of your tablet

Tap the one that's yours, enter the password in the box and then tap Connect. In the next screen, tap Next. On pages 70-72, we explain everything you need to know with regard to Wi-Fi and setting it up

4. **Add Your Account** – a Google account is an essential part of Android and this step lets you associate an existing account with the tablet, or create a new one. If you already have one, tap 'Existing' and enter your Google email address in the box and then the password

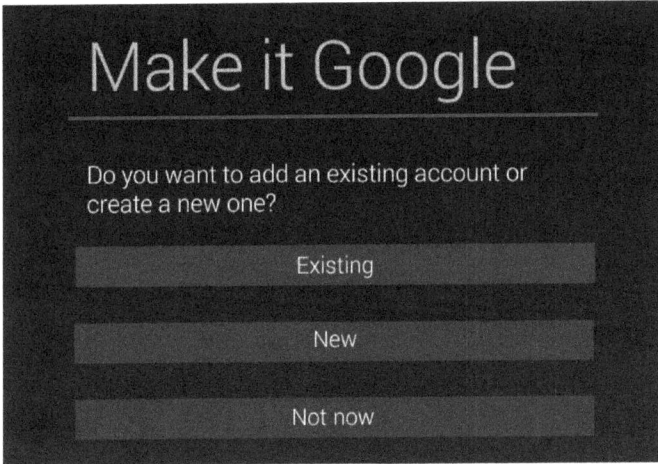

Otherwise, tap 'New' to set up a new account. We explain how to do this on pages 32-33

5. **Google Services** – the Google Services screen opens. Here, you can choose whether or not to backup the data on the tablet to your Google account (we recommend you do); and to receive communications regarding news and offers from Google Play

6. **Welcome Screen** – the Welcome screen appears. Tap Done to exit the setup wizard and go to your Home screen

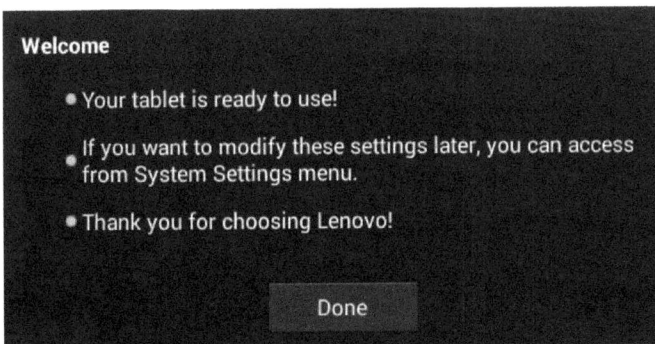

If you choose to skip any of the settings, they can be configured later on.

Set Up a Google Account

A Google account is almost mandatory with an Android tablet. It's not absolutely essential to have one but if you don't, you won't be able to download apps, games, movies, TV programs and other types of content. Neither will you be able to take advantage of Google services such as Calendar, Contacts and Back Up.

So if you skipped the option to create one when the setup wizard was running, we recommend that you do so now:

1. Tap the Home button to open the Home screen if you are not already on it. Then swipe to the left to open the Apps screen, which shows you all the apps installed on the tablet.

2. Find the Settings app and tap to open it

3. The Settings screen opens – tap Add Account in the Accounts section

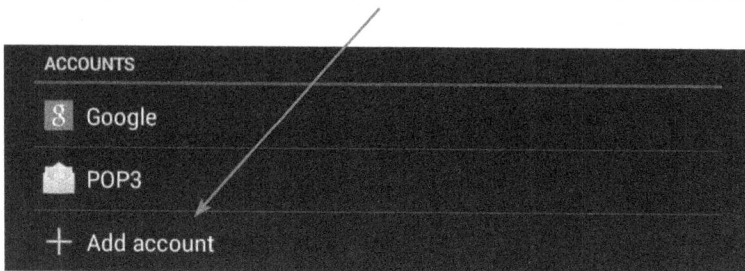

4. The 'Add an Account' window will open offering you a number of account options as shown on the right

5. Tap the Google option

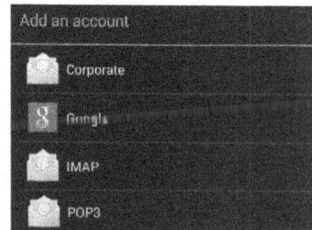

6. In the 'Add a Google account' screen, tap 'Existing' if you already have a Google account. Simply sign in by entering your email address and password. If you want to create a new account, tap 'New'

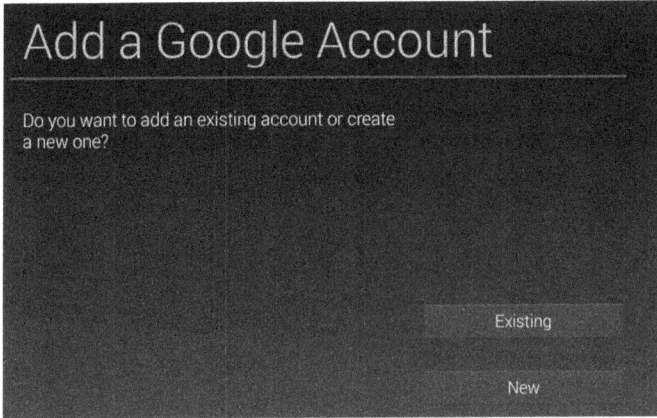

Add a Google Account

Do you want to add an existing account or create a new one?

Existing

New

7. You'll now see a series of prompts requesting your name, user-name, and a password. Then you'll see a recovery options screen that lets you backup your password in case you should ever forget it

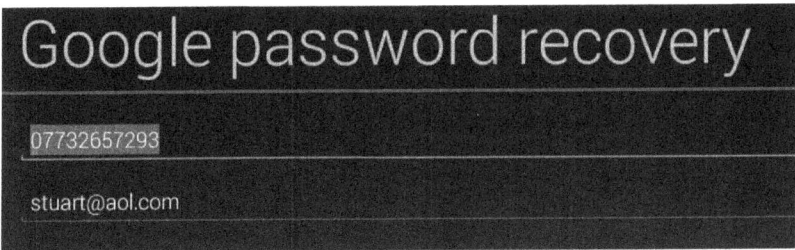

Google password recovery

07732657293

stuart@aol.com

Just enter a phone number and email address that you want the lost password to be sent to

8. Agree the Terms & Conditions by tapping 'I accept'

9. You will be asked to authenticate the account by entering a scrambled word

10. Finally, you are asked if you want to register a credit card with the account. You are under no obligation here but doing so saves you having to enter your card details every time you buy something

11. Your Google account is created

Multiple Users

The first person to set up an account as described on pages 32-33 is allocated the owner, or admin, account – this has complete control over the system.

Later versions of Android make it possible to also create separate accounts that other people can use. Additionally, restricted accounts can be created that limit what the user can do with the tablet.

To set up an account for another user:

1. On the Apps screen, tap Settings

2. Go the Device section – if the separate accounts feature is available, you'll see a Users entry. Tap it to access the settings screen

3. You will see two options: User and Restricted profile

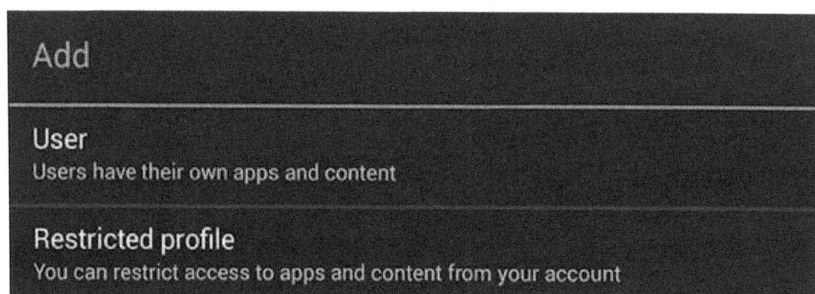

> ## Add
>
> ### User
> Users have their own apps and content
>
> ### Restricted profile
> You can restrict access to apps and content from your account

User Account

To create a standard user account, tap Users. With this option, the account holder has complete access to the tablet and its settings. Because of this, you, or they, will have to go through the full Google account creation process that you did when setting up your own account.

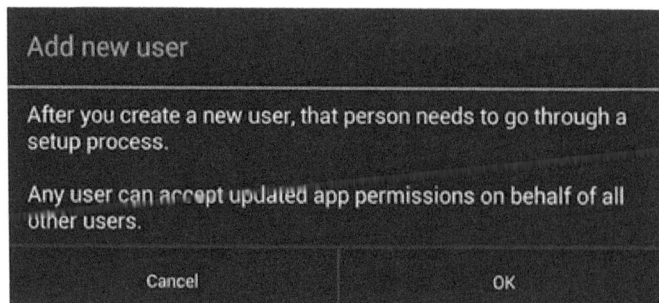

> ## Add new user
>
> After you create a new user, that person needs to go through a setup process.
>
> Any user can accept updated app permissions on behalf of all other users.
>
> | Cancel | OK |
> | --- | --- |

1. In the 'Add new user' screen, tap OK

cont'd

2. In the 'Set up user now?' screen, tap 'Set up now'

3 The user is now prompted to set up an account by entering his/her personal details

4. The user account is now created and the tablet switches to the Home screen of the new account. The user can now start using the tablet and has full access to everything on it

Restricted Profile Account

A restricted profile account is one that provides limited access to the tablet – settings and privileges are set by the owner of the device. Accounts of this type are intended for children or people who you don't trust with full access. To set up a Profile account:

1. Referring back to the top image on page 34, tap 'Restricted profile'

2. The next screen advises that you need to set a screen lock passcode with which to prevent the user of the profile account from accessing your data and apps. Tap SET LOCK

3. A screen opens offering three types of lock – a drawn pattern, a PIN number, or a password. Tap the one you want to use

4. Next, enter your pattern, PIN or password and tap Continue. You will be asked to confirm by entering it again. Then tap OK

5. You are now asked to specify which Notifications are to be shown when the device is locked – none, all, or specified. Then tap Done

6. In the final step, you are shown a list of all the apps on the tablet. By tapping a switch to the right of each app, you can enable or restrict access to each and every app

When you have set your restrictions, tap the Home button at the bottom of the screen to end the account setup procedure.

After both standard user and restricted profile user accounts have been set up, a button is placed on the Lock screen for the new user. All they have to do is tap on it to enter the tablet.

Date, Time, & Time Zone

You can let Android adjust the date and time automatically, or you can set it yourself. By default, the automatic option is selected but if you want to change this, follow these steps:

1. Access the Apps screen and then tap Settings

2. In the System section of the Settings app, tap 'Date & time'

3. In the 'Automatic date & time' screen, tap Off

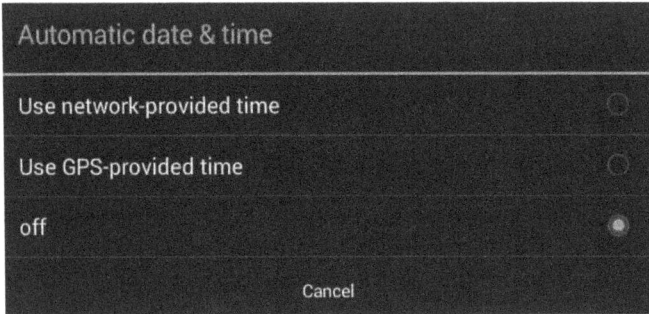

4. Tap the 'Set date' and 'Set time' options to enter the date and time manually. When finished, tap Done for each

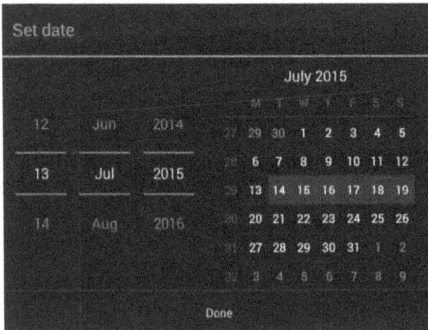

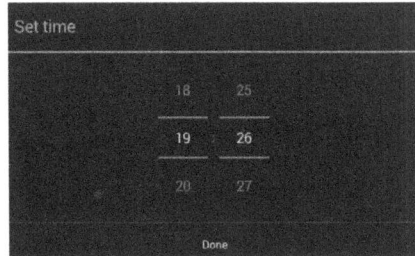

5. To change the time zone, tap 'Select time zone' and then choose from the list that opens

6. If you want to use the 24-hour time format, tap 'Use 24-hour format'

7. The final option in the Date & time settings lets you choose from a range of date formats

Brightness

The brightness of your tablet is important in more ways than one. Yes, it needs to be at a level that makes it possible to read what's on the screen but it also needs to be at a level that doesn't drain the battery too quickly.

Setting the Brightness

We'll look at how to set the brightness level first. There are actually two ways to do this:

- On the Apps screen, tap the Settings app. Then, in the Device section, tap Display. Under Display, you'll see the brightness setting. Tap it to open the Brightness control as shown below:

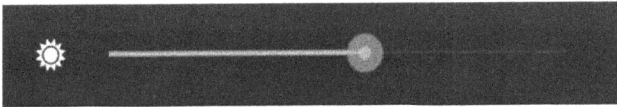

- The second, and quickest, way is to open the tablet's Quick Settings. Swipe down from the top-right of the screen and in the Quick Settings window, you'll see the brightness control

Brightness Apps

Another option is to download one of the many Brightness apps available in the Play Store – these provide many more features and controls.

For example, Lux is a third-party app that, amongst other things, lets you calibrate your tablet's light sensor, thus saving you battery power and reducing eye strain if your tablet is normally too bright in dark rooms.

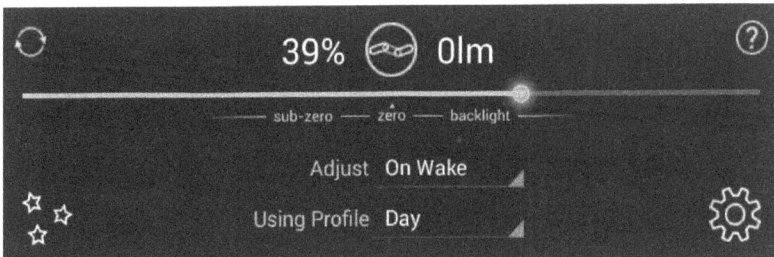

Probably the best feature of Lux (shown above) and apps like it, is its auto-brightness mode, which uses your tablet's light sensor. Once you've installed Lux, there's a tutorial that guides you through the setup and day-to-day use of the app.

Background

The background image on your tablet is known as wallpaper and, as it is quite likely that you won't particularly like the default image, it is just as well that it can be changed.

To do this:

1. Go to the Apps screen

2. Tap Settings

3. In the Device section, tap Display

4. In the Personalize section, tap Wallpaper

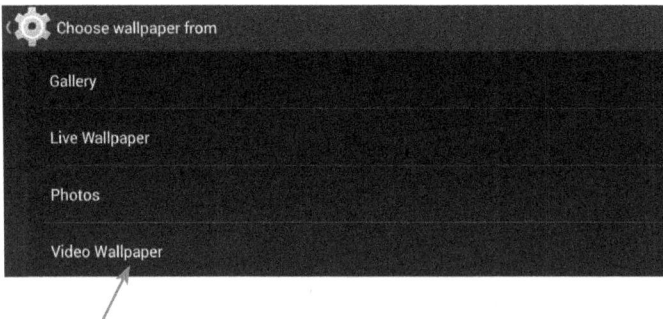

5. In the window that opens, you'll see four options:

Live Wallpaper
The Live Wallpaper option opens a list offering a choice of animated (moving) images:

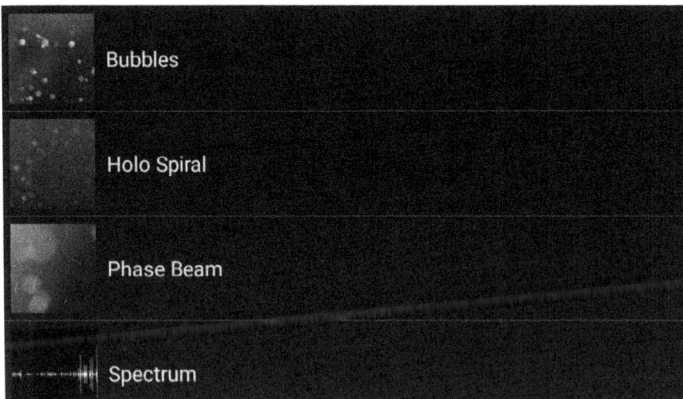

Tap one to see a preview of what it looks like – if you like it, tap 'Set Wallpaper' at the bottom of the screen.

Gallery/Photos

Tapping the Gallery and Photos options take you to the Gallery App and the Photos App respectively. Both are picture-related apps and will show you all the pictures on your tablet.

You can select any picture from them and set it as the tablet's wallpaper – it doesn't matter from which of the two apps you do it.

Video Wallpaper

The video wallpaper option lets you set any videos on the tablet as 'moving wallpaper'. Just select the required video and tap 'Set wallpaper'.

Lock Screen Wallpaper

Go back to the Personalize section of Display and you will see a 'Lock screen wallpaper' option. Tap this to open a screen showing a list of thumbnailed images.

Touch a thumbnail to see a preview of the wallpaper in the main part of the screen. To set it as wallpaper, tap 'Set wallpaper'.

Animated Backgrounds

Still on the wallpaper theme, there is an Android feature called Daydream. This provides animated backgrounds which are very similar to the screen-savers found in computers.

However, the Daydream backgrounds only appear on the tablet when it is either charging up or when it is docked to a computer. In other words, it provides a method of using what would usually otherwise be a blank screen. Furthermore, you can download apps from the Play Store that use Daydream to display many different kinds of useful information, e.g. weather, stocks and shares, etc.

Access the feature by opening the Settings app and tapping Display. You'll then see the Daydream feature. Open it and you'll see three options:

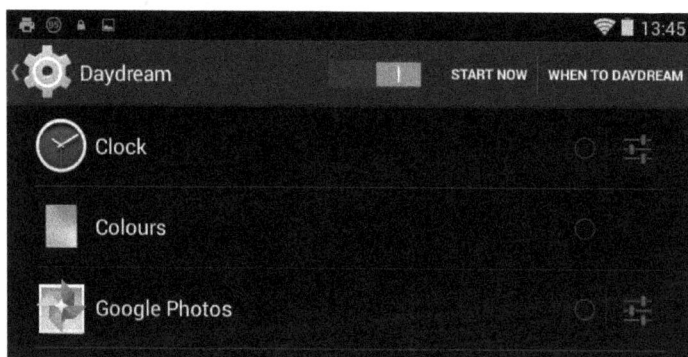

- **Clock** – select Clock to use the Daydream screen as either a digital or analog clock. You can also select Night mode, which dims the display. These options are available by tapping the gear icon

- **Colors** – tap Colors to create a multi-colored and ever changing background

- **Google Photos** – tap Google Photos and then tap the options button at the right to select which photos you want to display in a photo slide show. For example, you can choose pictures you have taken with the tablet's camera and pictures saved on Google Photos

Various options are available at the top-right of the screen. These let you turn the feature On or Off, activate Daydream immediately, and set when the feature is to work

Note that Daydream will start once the tablet has gone into Sleep mode. However, it won't display if you turn off the screen with the power button – you must let it go into Sleep mode on its own.

Putting Your Tablet to Sleep

We mentioned on page 37 that if the brightness level of a tablet's screen is set too high, the battery will be affected. Not only is this true, it actually places a greater load on the battery than any other part of the tablet.

The solution is to turn the screen off whenever it isn't being used. This can be done manually by pressing the power button once. However, it is too easy to forget to do this, so a much more effective method is to do it automatically. This is what a tablet's Sleep mode does – after a specified period of inactivity, it automatically removes the power to the screen thus turning it off.

By default, your tablet will come with Sleep mode enabled, and it is usually set to activate pretty quickly – far too quickly for many people. On most Android tablets, Sleep mode kicks in after only 15 seconds.

Fortunately, you can set a longer period:

1. Open the Settings app

2. In the Display section, tap Sleep – you will see the currently selected period as shown below

3. In the window that opens, select a more suitable period

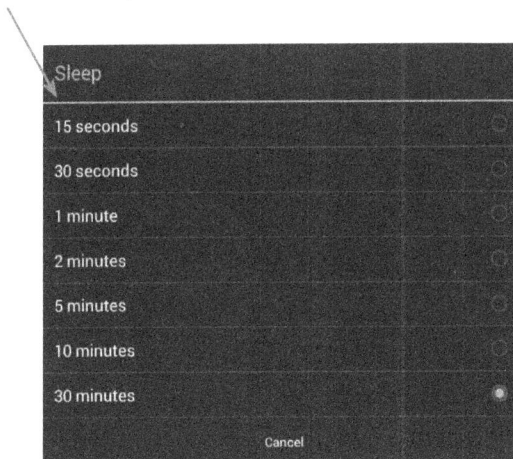

Now you can minimize the effects of the screen's brightness on the battery without having to be constantly pressing the power button to wake it up.

Sounds

The purpose of some apps is to keep you informed of various types of information as it comes in. News headlines, emails, text messages, and weather updates are typical examples. To bring these to your attention, the apps use visual notifications, some of which also sound an audible alert.

Just using your tablet also generates sounds, e.g. locking/unlocking the device and tapping keys on the virtual keyboard.

If you don't like hearing these sounds, want to change them, or change their volume level, you can do so in the tablet's sound settings options:

1. Tap the Settings app on the Apps screen

2. In the Device section, tap 'Audio profiles' and then tap the options button at the right of General

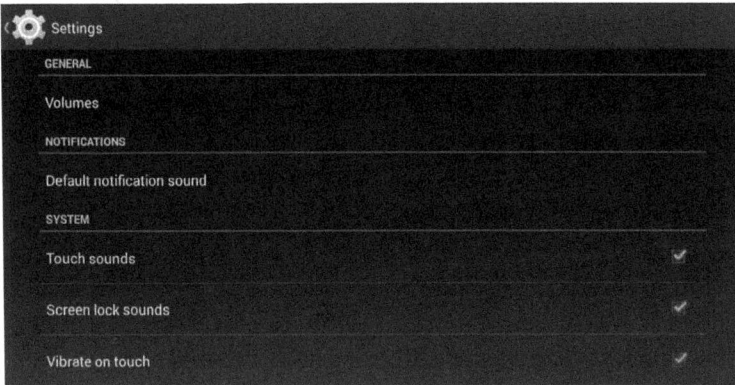

3. At the top, under General, tap Volumes. This lets you set the volume of both Notifications and alarms

4. Under Notifications, you can set a different sound for notification alerts

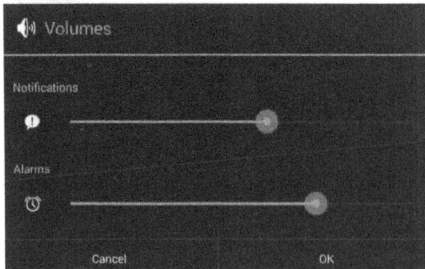

5. Further down, under System, are three controls: Touch sounds, Screen lock sounds, and Vibrate on touch. Touch sounds are the sounds made when you tap on the tablet's screen, Screen lock sounds is the sound made when you lock and unlock the tablet, and Vibrate on touch creates a very slight vibration whenever you touch the screen.

   All three options can be turned on or off here

Aids For The Handicapped

For users with disabilities that make it difficult to use a tablet, Android provides a number of accessibility features that can help considerably.

1. Open the Apps screen

2. Tap the Settings app

3. In the System section, tap Accessibility

You will now see all the accessibility options provided by your tablet as shown below:

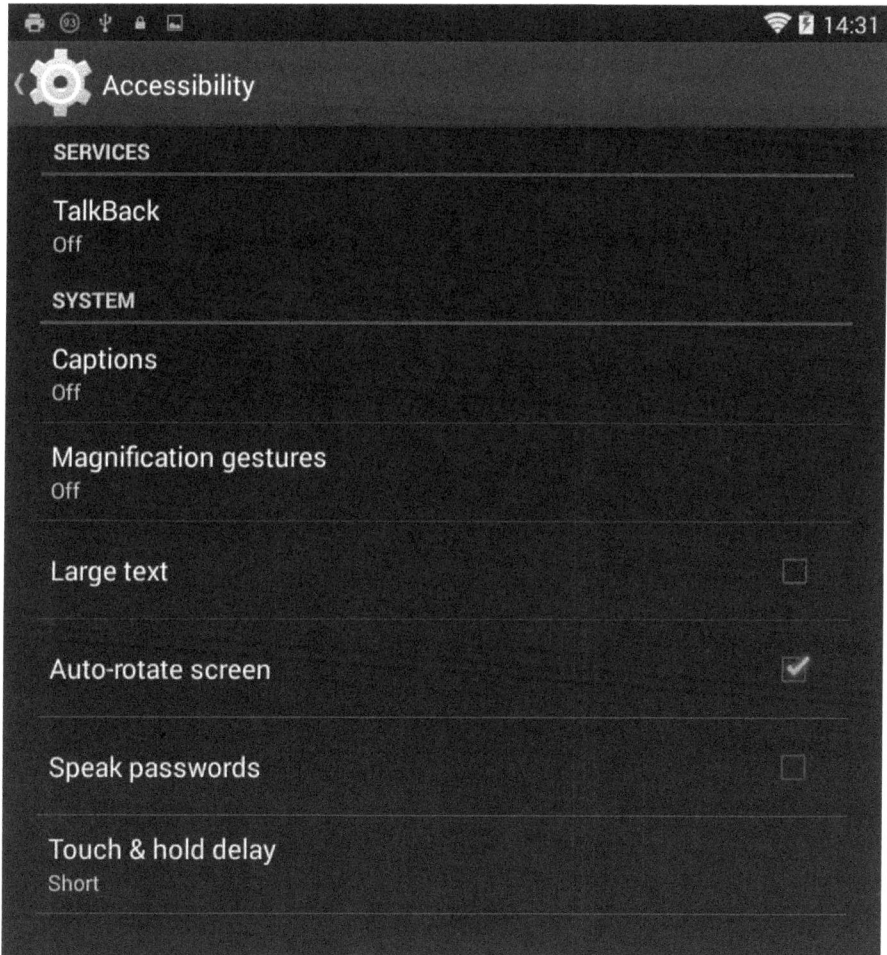

We'll take a brief look at what these options do and how they can be used to make it easier to use a tablet.

Talkback

Talkback is a built-in screen reader, and when it is turned on it provides audible information about what's on the screen, what you are touching and what's being activated. The feature is intended for users who have vision issues.

Captions

This feature enables a system-wide closed caption system for videos. It allows videos to display captions based on specified parameters that can be configured in the feature's settings. Configurable options include language, text size and caption style.

Magnification Gestures

Intended for those with poor eyesight, this feature lets you zoom in and out with the triple-tap gesture. Other gestures that can be used include the two-finger drag that lets you pan around the screen, and pinching or spreading two fingers to adjust the level of zoom.

It also makes it possible to temporarily magnify what you are touching by triple-tapping and holding. By continuing to hold, you can drag your finger to see different parts of the screen.

Large Text

A simple on/off control that enables a system-wide enlargement of text. You don't have any control over the size of the text though.

Auto-Rotate Screen

The Auto-rotate screen control lets you enable or disable the tablet's ability to automatically switch from Landscape mode to Portrait mode.

Speak Passwords

We mentioned the Talkback feature at the top of the page; well this setting controls TalkBack spoken feedback as you type passwords. When enabled, password characters are announced audibly as you type them, and when it is disabled, password characters are only audible via a headset.

Touch & Hold Delay

Intended for users with dexterity issues, this setting lets you set how long you need to press and hold to complete actions on the tablet.

You are given three options: Short, Medium and Long.

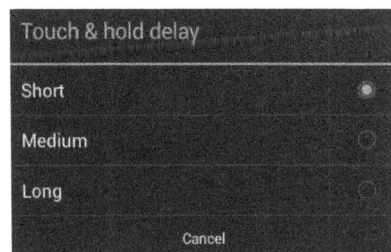

44

CHAPTER 4

The Keyboard

Your tablet does not come with a physical keyboard – this is one of the reasons the device is so small and portable. Instead, it is equipped with what's known as a 'virtual keyboard'.

In this chapter, we will see exactly how this virtual keyboard works and how you can set it up to suit your method of working. We explain how to enter and edit text, plus show you some very useful keyboard shortcuts that will save a lot of time and effort.

We also take a look at third-party keyboards and see how they can be used instead of the default tablet keyboard.

The Virtual Keyboard

As we mentioned in the introduction to this chapter, tablets do not provide a physical keyboard. Instead, in an effort to make them as compact and light as possible, they use an electronic, or virtual, version.

You won't actually see the keyboard until you open an app that requires text to be entered. Just tap in the text area of the app and the keyboard will slide up from the bottom of the screen; for example, a web page search box or an email message window.

For those of you not familiar with keyboards, it may be helpful to highlight certain of the keys at this point.

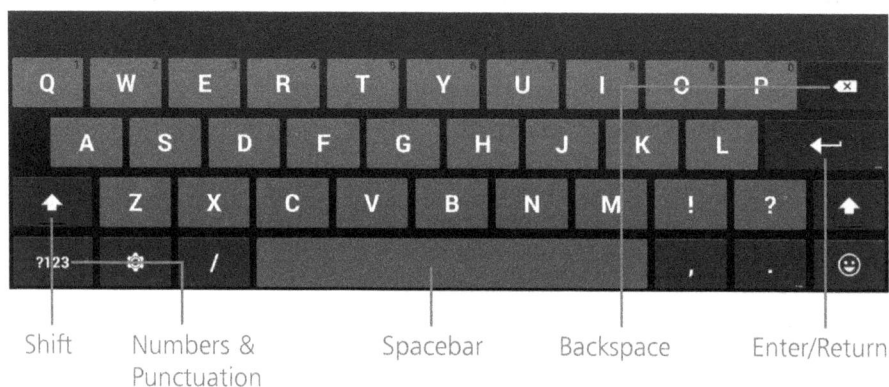

Shift   Numbers &   Spacebar   Backspace   Enter/Return
         Punctuation

Shift key – press this key to shift between upper-case and lower-case. When you have typed the upper-case character, the keyboard reverts to lower-case.

Double-tap the key for Caps Lock – you can easily tell when the lock is on as the letters on the keyboard are capitalized.

Numbers & Punctuation key – this key switches from letters, to numbers and punctuation marks. When in the latter mode, the Shift key turns into the Symbols key.

cont'd

Tap the Symbols key to access they Symbols keyboard as shown below:

Comma & Full Stop Keys – whatever screen you happen to be on, you will always find the Comma and Full Stop keys at the right of the Space bar.

Spacebar Key – the Space bar inserts a single space when tapped, two spaces when tapped twice, three spaces when tapped three times and so on.

Backspace Key – pressing this key deletes characters to the left of the cursor.

Enter/Return Key – press this key to end a paragraph of text and move the cursor to the next line. In a form, it will move the cursor to the next field.

Hide the Keyboard – there will be many occasions when you find the presence of the keyboard to be either unnecessary or just a nuisance. The solution is the Back button right at the bottom of the screen.

Whenever you open the keyboard, the Back button turns into a Down button. Tapping it removes the keyboard from the screen.

QWERTY Keyboard – to return to the standard QWERTY keyboard when you have finished with the numbers/punctuation and/or symbols screen, just tap the ABC key at the bottom-left of the keyboard.

As a final note, if you just cannot get on with your tablet's virtual keyboard, there is a wide range of physical keyboards that you can use instead. These connect to the tablet via Bluetooth and, while on the small side, they are far more tactile and conducive to long periods of intensive typing.

Text Entry

To enter text in an app, open it and tap once in a text field – this action will open the keyboard. All you have to do now is type in your text. As you do so, you will notice two things:

Predictive Text

Android's keyboard has a feature that attempts to predict what you are intending to type – this is known as Predictive Text. As you type, the feature offers three suggestions that it places in a bar at the top of the keyboard.

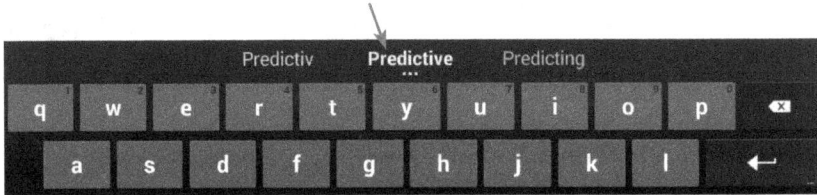

If you want to accept any of the suggestions, just tap on it. The feature can often save you from having to type out a long word in full; it's also handy when you are not sure how a word is spelled. For more suggestions, press and hold on any of the words and a list of related words will pop-up.

Spell Checking

The Android keyboard also has a built-in spell checker. Misspelled words are clearly underlined in red.

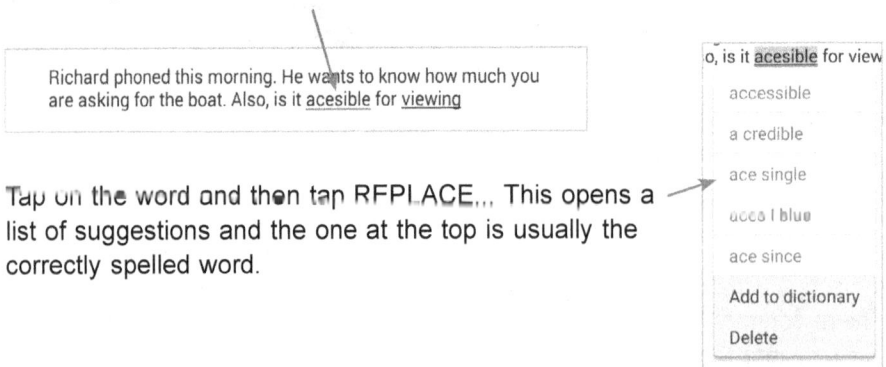

Tap on the word and then tap REPLACE... This opens a list of suggestions and the one at the top is usually the correctly spelled word.

Gesture Typing

Another method of entering text is provided by Android's Gesture Typing feature. With it, you can enter words by simply sliding your fingers from letter to letter and selecting the suggested words.

To type a word using gesture typing, follow these steps:

1. Tap in the text field to open the keyboard

2. Slide your finger slowly across the letters of the word that you want to input. To enter gold, for example, slide through the letter G, across to the letter O, across to L and then D, all the time keeping your finger on the screen. As your finger moves, you'll see a trail showing the path it has taken

   If there's a double letter in the word you are entering, just slide your finger over that letter as usual and the keyboard will suggest the word with the double letter

3. As your finger moves, a little pop-up window will follow it showing the letters you have swiped. When you see the required word in the window, take your finger off the screen

4. The word will now be entered in the text field

5. You will also see suggested words appear on the Predictive Text bar – just tap one to select it

6. When you use gesture typing, there's no need to use the space bar – just continue to slide your finger across the letters you want to input, then lift your finger to start the next word

A useful tip is to hold the tablet in Landscape mode when using gesture typing – this effectively enlarges the keyboard, thus creating more space between the keys for your finger to move about in.

To begin with, you may find gesture typing to be quite difficult. However, once you get the hang of it, it becomes progressively easier. In fact, experienced practitioners can use it with both hands.

As a general rule though, the feature is more suited to short messages, such as text messages and emails. Attempting to write long documents with it is not really practical.

By default, the feature is enabled. Should you wish to disable it, you can do so in the keyboard's settings. Open the Settings app, tap 'Language & input' and then tap the options button at the right of 'Google Keyboard'. Tap 'Enable gesture typing' to Off.

Dictating Text

If your hands aren't free – or you just feel lazy – you can enter words by speaking them rather than by typing. This is courtesy of the Dictation feature that can be activated by a microphone button on the keyboard.

Note that the feature is turned off by default – turn it on as follows:

1. Open the Settings app and tap 'Language & input'

2. Tap 'Google voice typing' to activate Dictation

Dictation works by sending your voice input to Google's speech recognition service, where it's examined, converted to text, and then sent back to your tablet. This means of course, that an Internet connection is required. Thanks to Google's massive computing power, the feature is very accurate.

However, even if an Internet connection is not available, Dictation will still work – it won't be as accurate though. It will also be necessary for the language being spoken to be actually installed on the tablet. By default, the only pre-installed language is English (US). If you require a different language, do the following:

1 Open the Dictation feature's settings as described above

2. Tap the options button at the right of 'Google voice typing'

3. Tap 'Offline speech recognition'

4. Tap All, tap the language you want to install and then tap DOWNLOAD in the pop-up window

The language will now be downloaded and automatically installed after which it will be available for selection.

To enter punctuation marks while using dictation, just say period, comma, question mark, or exclamation mark. Android will enter the appropriate punctuation mark instead of the words.

Working With Text

Editing text on a tablet is never going to be as quick as on a computer or laptop. Nevertheless, it's surprising what is possible.

Positioning the Cursor

Getting the cursor precisely where you want it is an essential part of text editing. To do it, tap as near to the desired place as possible – a blue marker will appear just below.

Richard phoned this morning about the boat. He wants to

Then place your finger on the marker and drag it to where the cursor is to be positioned.

Selecting Text

To select an individual word, double-tap on it. It will be highlighted and markers placed on either side of it.

Richard phoned this morning about the boat. He wants to

Richard phoned this morning about the boat. He wants to

To select a block of text, drag the markers left and right, and up and down. The selected text will be highlighted in blue.

Moving & Copying Text

Select the text to be moved or copied as described above. At the top of the screen, you"ll now see the Options bar shown below. Tap CUT or COPY.

✓ DONE   Text selection   ⠿ SELECT ALL   ✂ CUT   ▢ COPY

Tap where the text is to be placed and then tap Paste. This can be in the current page or even a different app – just open the app, tap where you want the text to go and a Paste option will appear – tap it to paste the text.

Richard phoned about the boat.He wants to

PASTE   REPLACE...

Note that many apps that allow you to enter text will offer a toolbar that includes a Paste option – this can be used to paste copied text.

Keyboard Tricks & Shortcuts

There are a number of tricks and shortcuts that can be used with the Android keyboard. For people who do serious amounts of text entry, these can be extremely useful:

Quickly redo incorrect keystrokes
When you tap a key nothing is entered until your finger leaves the screen. So if you hit the wrong key, just keep your finger on the screen and slide it across to the correct one.

Quickly insert numbers & punctuation
To insert numbers and punctuation, you press the .?123 key, press the required character and then tap the ABC key to revert to the letters keyboard.

A quicker way is to press the .?123 key but instead of releasing it and going to the required character, keep your finger on the screen and slide it to the key you want. When it has been selected, release the key and the keyboard will automatically revert to letters.

More quick punctuation
Swiping up on the Comma key will insert an apostrophe; swiping up on the Period key inserts a quotation mark.

Quick capital letters
Rather than engage the Shift key every time you need to type a capital letter, just press and hold the Shift key and drag your finger to the letter you want to capitalize

Related characters
Pressing and holding a character will, in many cases, open a list of related characters above the key. For example, other currencies from the Currency key and accented versions of letter keys.

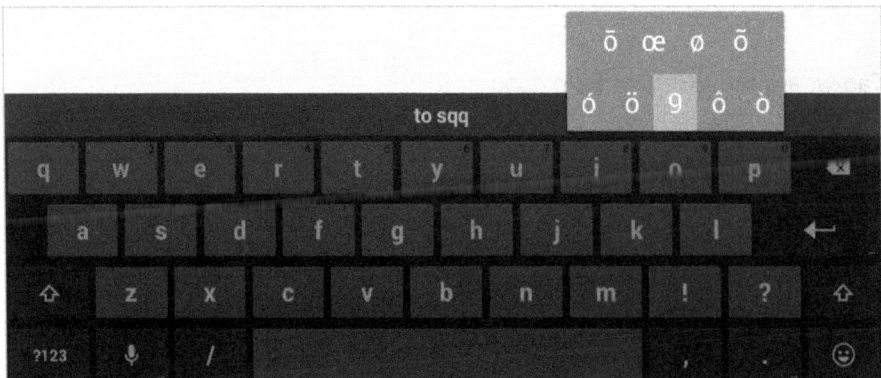

Emoticons

Also known as smileys and emojis, emoticons provide more of a fun feature rather than serve any practical purpose. Basically, they let you convey your feelings or tone while writing a message.

To insert emoticons in your emails and text messages, press the Emoticon key at the bottom-right of the keyboard next to the Full Stop key.

This opens a categorized list of hundreds of icons and emoticons as shown below. Select from the categories or swipe to the right to view them all.

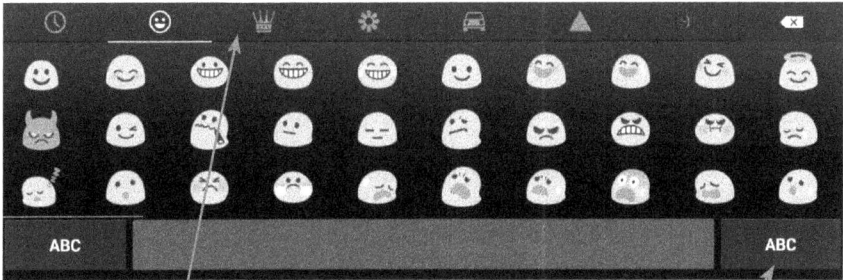

Emoticon categories   Tap to return to standard keyboard

Quick Spacing

To quickly end a sentence and at the same time start a new one, double-tap the space bar. This ends the current sentence with a full stop and adds a space ready for the beginning of the new one.

Phrase Shortcuts

If you type a certain phrase or sentence frequently, you can set a shortcut for it which, when typed, automatically expands to the full phrase.

To set this up:

1. Tap the Settings app on the Apps screen and in the Personal section of Settings, tap 'Language & input'

2. Tap 'Personal dictionary'

3. Tap Add at the top-right of the screen

4. In the top field, type your phrase and in the bottom field, the shortcut

5. Test it works by opening the keyboard and typing the shortcut. In a bar at the top of the keyboard, you will see the phrase – tap to select it

Setting Up The Keyboard

A wide range of settings are available for your tablet's virtual keyboard. These enable you to configure it to suit your way of working and to turn off features that you don't need or just find annoying. These can be accessed by tapping 'Language & input' in the Settings app. Some you may be interested in include:

Spell Checker
On by default, you can disable the Spell Checker by tapping on it to uncheck the checkbox. Tap the options button at the right and you will be able to specify the language used by the spell checker.

Personal Dictionary
We mentioned the Personal dictionary on the previous page and explained how it can be used to create phrase shortcuts. Well, it can also be used for another purpose and this is to modify Android's auto-correction feature.

Whenever you're entering text on your Android tablet, the auto-correction feature will correct any words it thinks you have spelled incorrectly. Unfortunately, it doesn't always get it right – sometimes, you type a word that you know is correct (maybe a product or service) and Android insists on changing the word.

To prevent this, you can use the Personal dictionary – it lets you manually add (and remove) words that you don't want Android to automatically change.

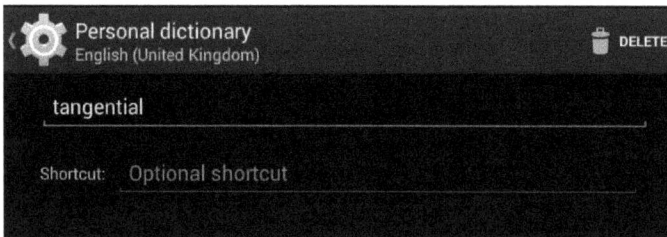

Tap Personal Dictionary to open it and then tap the + sign at the top-right. Enter all the words that you don't want Android to correct automatically.

Google Keyboard
The Google Keyboard setting is where you will find most of your tablet's keyboard settings. Tap the options button at the far-right to open them:

- **Input languages** – this setting lets you specify the language used by the keyboard. To change it, you will need to first deselect the 'Use system language' option at the top of the screen

- **General** – three settings are available here: the first setting is 'Auto-capitalization' – this capitalizes the first word of each sentence; the second is 'Vibrate on keypress' – you'll feel a slight vibration when you type a letter; and the third is 'Sound on keypress' – this turns the sound on or off

- **Add-on dictionaries** – this lets you add extra dictionaries to your tablet. Just tap the required dictionary and an Install button will appear at the far-right – tap it to install the dictionary

- **Auto-correction** – we've already mentioned that when typing on an Android tablet, your spelling is checked automatically and replacement words are suggested. This feature can be useful at times, but it can also be a hindrance.

  Fortunately, it's easy to adjust the aggressiveness of the feature or to turn it off completely. Tap Auto-correction and you can select from four options: Off, Modest, Aggressive, and Very aggressive

- **Show correction suggestions** – Android places words it thinks are relevant to what is being typed on a bar at the top of the keyboard. If you don't want to see these, you can disable the feature here

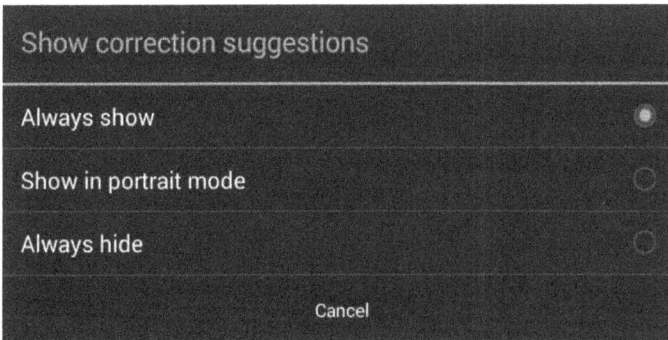

- **Advanced** – this setting lets you access miscellaneous settings. For example, you can set the keypress sound volume, the key long press delay, the keypress vibration duration, and access to the keyboard's emoticon palette

Alternatives to The Default Keyboard

As with all of your tablet's default apps, there are many alternatives available at the Play Store. So if for some reason you don't like the keyboard supplied with your tablet, you can easily replace it.

Three of the best are:

SwiftKey
One of SwifyKey's best features is its superb predictive text engine that learns from the way you type and offers better word and spelling suggestions as a result. It will learn from your emails, social networks, text messages, etc, in order to auto-fill your friends names, addresses, favorite words, and more.

SwiftKey also provides multiple keyboard layouts, multiple keyboard sizes, tablet-friendly layouts that you can move around the screen, themes, personalization options, and cloud syncing. It also supports gesture typing and swipe-to-type, including its 'Flow through Space' feature, which lets you type entire sentences without lifting your finger.

Swype
Swype's main claim to fame is its swipe-to-type engine that lets you swipe words or even complete sentences. It also provides an excellent predictive text engine, crowd-sourced dictionaries, and customization options.

Other features include split-keyboard options, tablet-friendly layouts, speech recognition, smooth typing, and easy language switching. Swype also makes it easy to add punctuation and copy and paste text, by swiping key shortcuts. For visually impaired users, Swype taps into Android's Accessibility features for TalkBack and Explore By Touch.

Fleksy
The Fleksy keyboard is all about speed and extremely high accuracy. It uses the standard QWERTY layout as standard but when you start typing, the layout of the keyboard changes so that the letters you need next are right there next to your finger. Once you have a feel for where to put your fingers, Fleksy lets you type words and entire sentences without even looking at the keyboard.

It also provides an exceptional auto-correction engine that is good enough to correct a word to the one you intended even if you've mistyped every single letter. Other features include customizing options for keyboard size and transparency, auto-punctuation, and multiple themes.

CHAPTER 5

Your Tablet's Software

In Chapter Five, we take a look at the business end of your tablet – its software, or apps, as they are commonly known. We explain what the pre-installed apps do, show how to use Google's Play Store to get more apps, and how to keep them updated.

We also see how to manage your apps in termsof organization so as to make the most efficient use of the tablet. This includes how to create and use extra folders – something that is not immediately obvious.

Software

Apps

By itself your tablet is just a piece of hardware – well designed and constructed – but still just a piece of hardware. To do something useful, it requires instructions. On a computer, these instructions are provided by software programs, most of which are highly complex, large in size (which means they can take a long time to install and configure), and require a considerable amount of system resources to run. Computer software can also be expensive.

The app is the tablet equivalent of computer software. However, due to the power and system resource restraints placed on tablets by their reliance on battery power, and small physical size, the software used on them needs to be similarly restricted in terms of power and resource requirements.

Thus, in general, apps for tablets and smartphones are much more streamlined than their computer equivalents. They are small in size, quick to download and install, and very inexpensive. The downside is that currently, they provide limited options and are restricted to simple tasks.

Tablets are supplied with a number of pre-installed apps that provide basic functionality, such as email, an Internet browser and photography. To increase the capability of your tablet, you can of course download other apps from the Play Store as we'll see later.

Widgets

Widgets are basically 'mini-apps' that perform a simple function, such as providing a weather report or stock quote. They provide an 'at-a-glance' view of an app's most important data and functionality right from the tablet's Home screen. Typically, they fall into one of the following categories:

- **Information** – information widgets display information elements that are important to a user and track how that information changes over time. For example, the weather, clocks, stock quotes, etc

- **Collection** – these widgets display elements of the same type, such as a collection of pictures from a photos app

- **Control** – control widgets let you access frequently used functions right from the Home screen without having to open the app itself

- **Hybrids** – basically, Hybrids are widgets that combine elements of the Information, Collection and Control widget types

Widgets are located on your tablet's Apps screen, and most can be re-sized thus providing a means of setting the amount of content they display.

Apps Supplied With Your Tablet

To see the apps pre-installed on your tablet, tap the Apps button on the Favorites bar or swipe to the right – this opens the Apps screen:

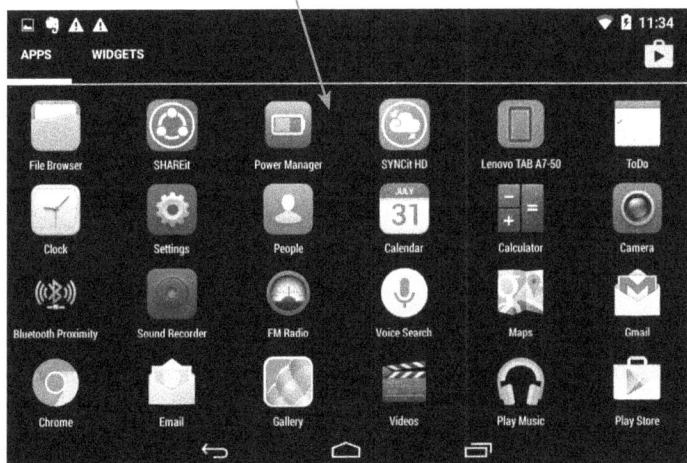

The default view as shown above shows all the pre-installed apps. To see the widgets, tap WIDGETS at the top-left of the screen.

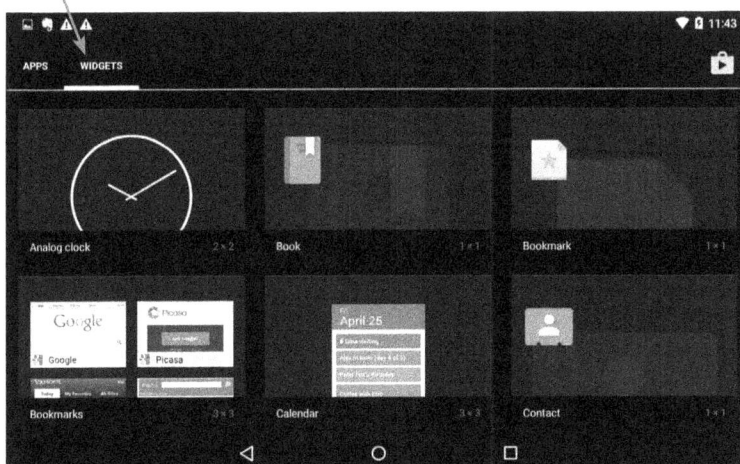

Lets take a look at the pre-installed apps typically found on Android tablets.

While the apps listed on this page and the next are standard on virtually all Android tablets, manufacturers often include a few of their own. Often, these are of limited use and are the first apps the user uninstalls.

Calculator – a basic calculator that also provides some scientific functions. There are many better and more featured calculators at the Play Store

Calendar – typical of all digital calendars, the Calendar app lets you make and store appointments etc. By synchronizing the app with Google Cloud, your appointments can also be viewed and edited on other Android devices. This can be a very useful feature

Camera – the camera app provides access to the camera, or cameras, supplied with your tablet

Chrome – if your tablet has the Chrome app, this is what you will use to browse the Internet. Some tablets will provide other browsers though

Clock – by default, the Clock app shows you the current date and time in your location. Other functions include an alarm, a stopwatch and a timer

Docs – with Google Docs, you can create and share documents, including Microsoft Word documents. An offline mode is provided for when an Internet connection is not available

Drive – the Google Drive app stores all your files safely online so they cannot be lost. They will also be accessible on other Android devices

Email – an important app, Email lets you send and receive email, add and manage email accounts

Gmail – the Gmail app lets you create a Google Gmail account, or use an existing one. The app is much the same as the Email app mentioned above and provides similar features

Google – searching your tablet and the Internet is an important function and this is provided by the Google app. It also lets you set up Google Now

Google + – for social media aficionados, this app lets you share various types of content with other people. For example: pictures and videos

Google Settings – not really an app as such, this is basically a collection of shortcuts to the various settings screens for your Google account

Hangouts – this app lets you communicate with friends and family by phone or by text

Maps – discover exactly where you are, find locations, and get directions with Google Maps – possibly one of the most useful apps on your tablet

Gallery – the Gallery app provides a number of picture-related functions. These include organizing, finding, backing up, and sharing

People – the People app is your address book where you can keep contact details of the people in your life, addresses and more

Photos – some tablets will have the Photos app as well as the Gallery app. This does much the same thing but has less features

Play Books – this app lets you read ebooks on your tablet. Other functions include browsing the Play Store for new books and managing them

Play Games – play the latest games, discover and download new games, compete in multi-player games, track achievements, plus much more

Play Movies & TV – with this app, you can play movies and TV programs purchased from the Play Store

Play Music – the Play Music app is used to play music, and buy and download music from the Play Store. You can also use it to copy music to your tablet from a computer

Play Newsstand – very similar to the Play Books app, this lets you buy and read magazines on your tablet

Play Store – the Play Store is a central location for all the various types of content that can be purchased and downloaded to your tablet, e.g. books, music, etc

Settings – both your tablet and the apps on it can be customized and configured in many ways. The Settings app is where it is done and it will probably be one of the most used apps on your tablet

Voice Search – the Voice Search app lets you do things with voice commands. For example: search queries, opening apps, performing tasks

YouTube – tapping this app takes you directly to the YouTube video sharing website

Where to Get Apps From

As we have just seen, your tablet comes with a good range of built-in apps that allow you to do all the things these devices are commonly used for. However, if you need more or better apps, or a type of app not supplied with the tablet, the Play Store is the place to go.

To do it:

1. Open the Apps screen

2. Tap Play Store

3. The Play Store home screen opens. At the top, you'll see six category buttons These let you search for content by type

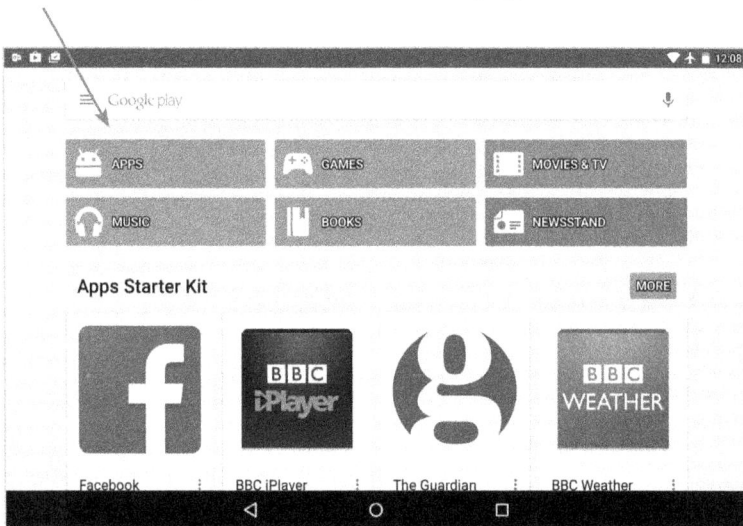

4. To see what a category has to offer, tap on its button. You will now see more buttons at the top of the screen

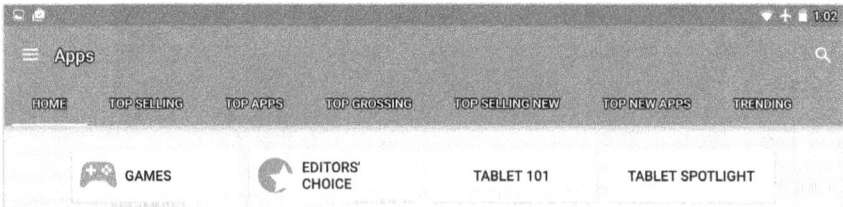

5. At the left is Categories – tap this to open a list of app genres. Other options are Home, Top Selling, Top Apps, Top Grossing, Top Selling New, Top New Apps and Trending

cont'd

6. Below the category buttons on the home screen, you'll see recommended items across a range of genres. Swipe down to view them all. An example is Word Games, as shown below:

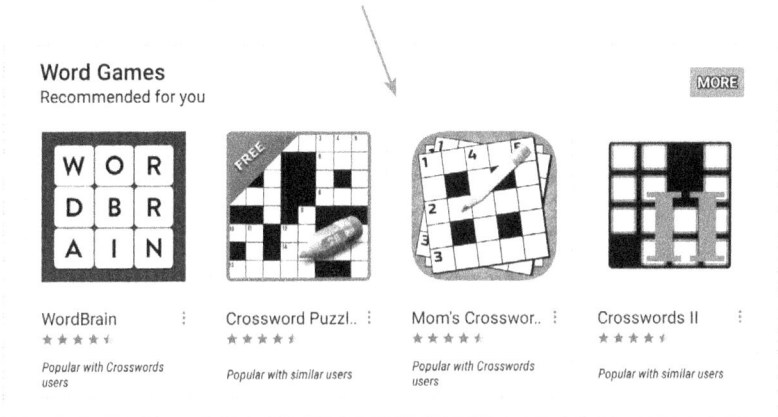

7. An alternative method of finding content is provided by the Search function, which you'll find at the top of the screen:

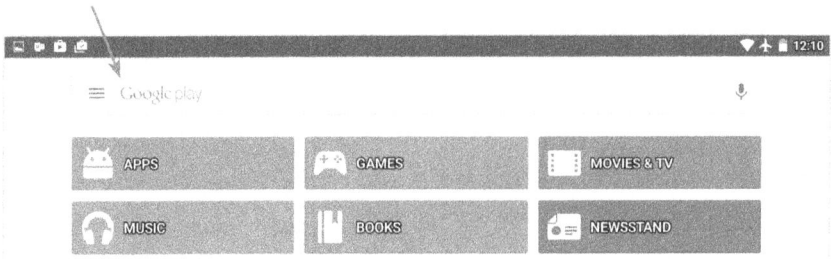

8. Enter your search query and then either tap on one of the suggestions that opens in a window below, or tap the magnifying glass button on the keyboard

9. At the left of the Search box, tap this ☰ button to open a list of more options.

    These include 'Store home' that takes you to the Play Store's home screen, 'My apps' that shows the apps you have installed, 'My wishlist' that lets you add items you may want to download at some point, and 'My account' that lets you add a payment method and also view your order history

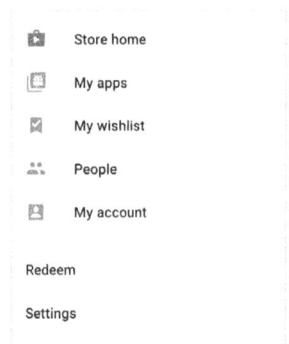

Reviewing & Installing Apps

Having found an app that may suit your purpose, you then need to take a closer look at what if offers, particularly if it comes with a price tag attached.

The way to evaluate an app is:

1. Tap on the app to open it

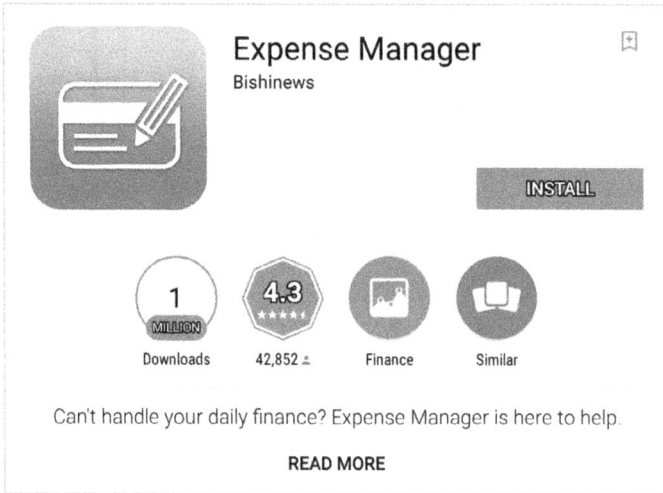

2. Towards the top of the screen, you'll see a Downloads icon and, next to it, the average review rating the app has received from other users. Tap the latter to open the list of reviews

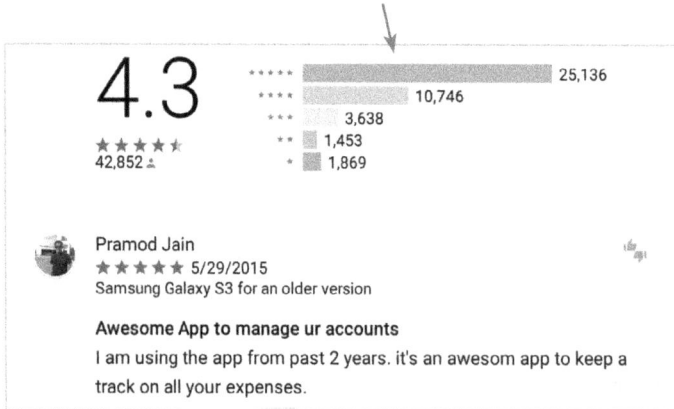

High download figures for an app suggest it is popular and thus good for its stated purpose. The reviews given to the app by other users are the best indicator of its quality though.

cont'd

3. Further down, you'll see a READ MORE link. Tap this to open a window that should explain in detail what the app does, and specify any hidden charges or in-app purchases

4. Below the READ MORE link, you will see some image thumbnails taken from the app. Tap to open them in a full-screen preview

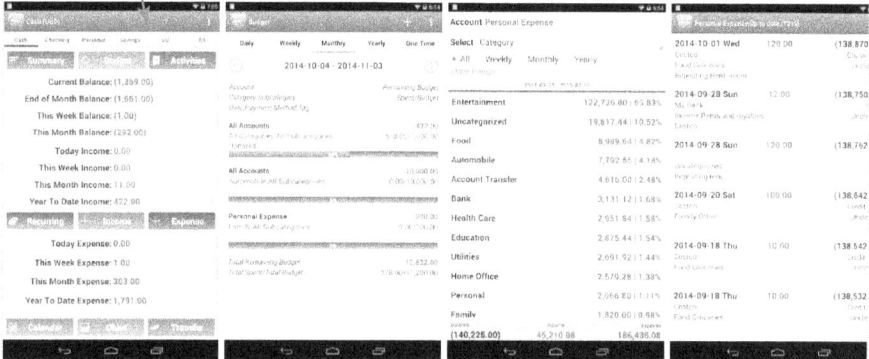

5. If you decide you want the app, tap the INSTALL button. This opens a window that specifies the permissions required by the app. It may, for example, need to access your Contacts list. Approve the requested permissions by tapping the Accept button

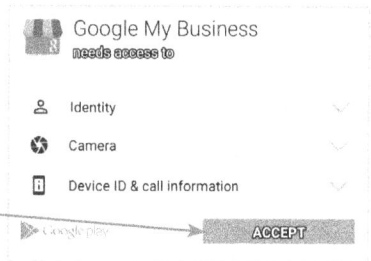

6. The app will now be downloaded to your tablet and then automatically installed. During the download, you will see a progress indicator

7. To locate your newly installed app, open the Apps screen where you will find it listed in alphabetical order. Tap to open it

8. Many apps need to be paid for. In this case, you will see the price of the app in the Install button as shown on the right

9. Tap the button and tap Accept in the next window to approve the permissions. If you haven't yet added a payment method to your tablet, you will now see a 'Payment Methods' window. Select the required option and fill in your details

10. When you have set up your payment method, payment will be taken for the app and it is then downloaded to your tablet

Keeping Your Apps Updated

Many of the apps on your tablet are under continuous development by their respective manufacturers. This is done to improve and further the apps performance and functionality. These improvements are administered in the form of updates, and they can be added either manually or automatically:

Manual Updates

To update your apps manually, open the Play Store as previously described. Then proceed as follows:

1. At the left of the Search box, tap the ☰ button

2. Tap 'My Apps' and then tap INSTALLED

3. To apply all the current updates in one go, tap the UPDATE ALL button

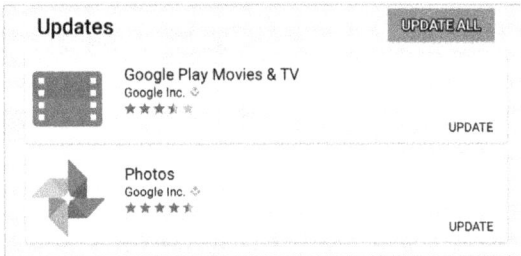

4. To update them individually, tap the UPDATE button to the right of each app to be updated. This opens the app – tap the UPDATE button again

Automatic Updates

A quicker way of keeping your apps updated is to configure the Play Store to add them automatically as and when they become available. To do this:

1. Tap the ☰ button to open the Options menu and then tap Settings

2. In the General section, tap 'Auto-update apps'

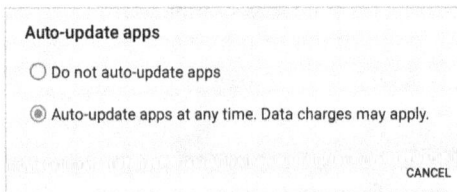

3. Tap the Auto-update option. Note that with some tablets this option is enabled by default. Once done, you can then forget about app updates – it will be done for you behind the scenes

App Management

Reordering Apps and Widgets

By default, your apps and widgets are located on the Apps screen (you may in fact have more than one App screen, depending on how many apps you have). In order to make the most efficient use of your tablet's screen space, you can rearrange the apps both by reordering their position on any screen and/or by moving them to a different screen.

To do this:

1. Open the Apps screen containing the app to be moved

2. Press and hold the app. To move it to a different position on the current screen, simply drag it to where you want it to go and then release it. The app it replaces will move down

3. To move an app to a different App screen or to the Home screen, press and hold as above and then drag it to the left or right side of the screen. The adjoining screen will open – position the app and release it

Creating App Folders

As you install more apps on your tablet, more App screens will be automatically created to accommodate them all. The more apps and thus App screens you have, the more difficult it is to find them.

The solution to this problem is to create app folders and place related apps inside them. For example, all your communication apps such as email, social media, messaging, etc, can be placed in one dedicated folder.

To do this:

1. Press and hold on one app and drag it onto another app

2. Release the app – the two app icons will merge into one creating a folder. You can add more apps if you want to

3. Initially, the folder is given the name 'Folder'. To change this to something more meaningful, tap the folder to open it

4. Tap 'Unnamed Folder' at the bottom. The keyboard opens allowing you to give the folder a name. In the example on the right, we have created a folder in which to place email-related apps, and named it Email

5. Should you subsequently wish to remove an app from a folder, just open the folder and drag the app out of it

Removing & Uninstalling Apps/Widgets

Removing an App or Widget

There will be occasions when you want to merely remove an app or widget from its current screen rather than uninstall it. The way to do this is to create an app screen specifically for this purpose and move the app to it – out of sight, out of mind as the saying goes!

Uninstall an App

On other occasions you will want to want to completely remove an app from your tablet, i.e. uninstall it. If it's an app you have downloaded from the Play Store, this is easy to do.

1. Press and hold the app to be deleted until you see an X at the top-left corner – just tap the X to open an Uninstall screen

2. Tap OK to uninstall the app

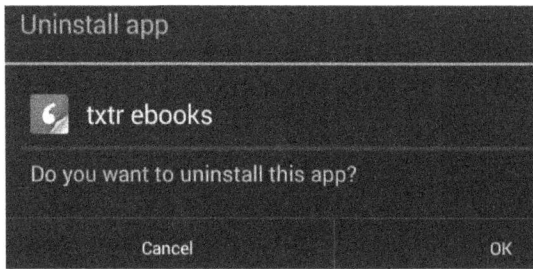

However, a number of the pre-installed apps cannot be uninstalled – the best you will be able to do is disable them. Should you wish to do this, proceed as follows:

1. Open the Apps screen and then tap the Settings app

2. In the Device section, tap Apps

3. Place your finger at the right of the Apps screen and flick it to the left to scroll across to the 'All' view

4. Locate the app to be disabled and tap it

5. You will see a DISABLE button at the right – tap it and then tap OK to confirm

CHAPTER 6

Getting Connected

Your Android tablet can do many things that do not require it to be connected a network. However, the device offers so much more when it is. For example: browsing the Internet, downloading content such as apps, music, video, books and magazines; sending and receiving email and text messages; and navigation with apps such as Maps. Not to mention of course, the currently extremely popular pastime of social media such as Facebook, YouTube, etc.

In this chapter, we explain everything you need to know with regard to networks and getting your tablet online.

Types of Connection

Your tablet will be either a Wi-Fi only model or a cellular model that can connect not just to Wi-Fi but also to cellular data networks, such as 3G and 4G. If you're not sure what model you have, open the Settings app and look at the 'Wireless & networks' section at the top of the screen.

Under Wireless & networks, tap More. If you now see a Cellular networks setting, your tablet is a cellular model.

Wi-Fi

A Wi-Fi only tablet can only connect to the Internet via a wireless, or Wi-Fi signal. These signals are produced by a device called a router that typically has a range of approximately 150 feet indoors and 300 feet outdoors.

Many homes have these routers installed as part of their broadband setup, and they are also widely found in public places such as airports, libraries and Internet Cafes. The latter are known as Wi-Fi hotspots and they enable people to use their tablets and smartphones while on the move.

The big advantage of Wi-Fi is that if you use your tablet at home, your connection is free as you're using the Wi-Fi network produced by your own router. Some public places offer free Wi-Fi hotspots but most don't, in which case you have to pay for your connection.

However, if you are in an area where Wi-Fi is not available, you won't be able to access the Internet, send/receive email, and you'll find that any apps that rely on Internet access will not work.

Cellular

Cellular tablets, on the other hand, can connect to the Internet wherever there is cellular network coverage in the same way that cell phones do. This is their big advantage and one that is much valued by people who travel a lot.

Furthermore, by installing a suitable app such as Skype (available from the Play Store), a cellular tablet can also be used as a phone (assuming you don't mind holding a tablet to your ear!).

Cellular tablets are designed to access a large frequency spectrum. This means they will work well in most locations globally that offer a cellular service.

Needless to say of course, there is a downside – namely cost! Cellular tablets are considerably more expensive than the Wi-Fi models. Not only that, you will also need to pay for a data service plan. This is essentially the same as the plan you buy for your cell phone and is subject to the same data restrictions and costs.

Setting Up a Wi-Fi Connection

When you first set up your tablet (as described on pages 30-31), you are asked to configure it to use a Wi-Fi network. The network you will use is the one generated by your home broadband router.

However, before you can, you need two pieces of information about it – its identifying name and its password. To get this, find your router and look at the rear of the case – you will see something similar to that below:

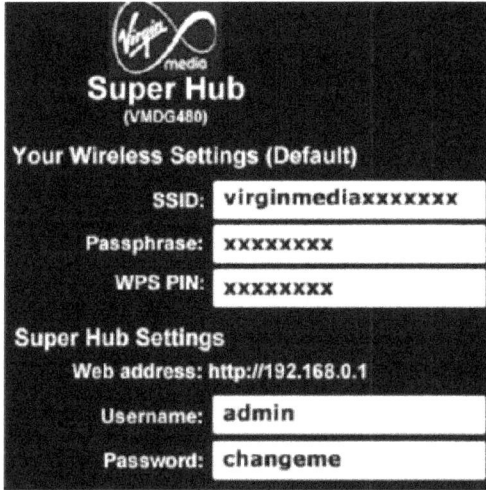

Make a note of the SSID number, which identifies the network and the passphrase or password. When the setup wizard asks for the password, enter it in the box, tap Connect – you're done.

If you chose not to set up Wi-Fi during the setup wizard, the procedure for doing it later on is:

1. On the tablet, open the Apps screen and then tap the Settings app

2. Under 'Wireless & networks', tap WLAN

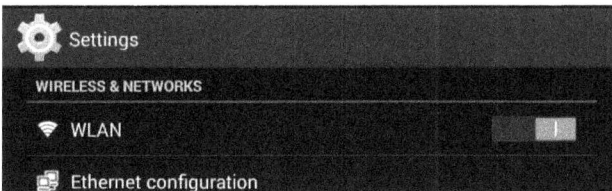

3. You will now see a list of all the Wi-Fi networks that are within range of your tablet as shown on the next page

cont'd

4. Tap your home Wi-Fi network (identified by the SSID number)

5. Enter the password or passphrase

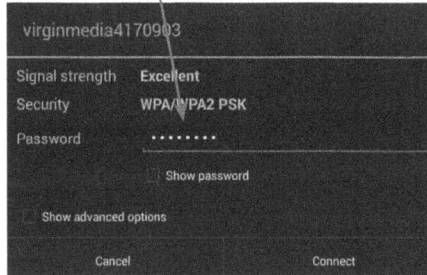

6. Tap the Connect button. Your tablet will now attempt to connect to the specified network. When a connection has been established, the word 'Connected' will appear below the network

Note that, henceforth, whenever your tablet is in range of your home network, it will automatically login to it – you won't have to select it (and enter the password) every time.

When using your tablet away from home, in a hotel for example, you can use the hotel's Wi-Fi by following steps 4 to 6. Note that many public places now provide free Wi-Fi so a password may not need to be entered.

Setting Up a Cellular Connection

Overview

To start, a brief overview of cellular networks may be helpful as it can be a confusing topic. This is due to the fact that cellular networks use a number of different technologies, the latest being 4G (4th Generation). This is gradually replacing the older, and less capable, 3G (3rd Generation) technology, which in turn replaced EDGE (2.75G) technology.

To complicate things further, there are several different implementations of each type. For example, there are three types of 4G network – LTE, HSPA+ and WiMax. However, regardless of the minor differences between them, they all do essentially the same thing – provide data transfer rates that are some 10 times faster than 3G. Furthermore, 4G networks have the potential to provide even faster speeds in years to come.

Which type of cellular network your tablet connects to depends on your geographic location. In advanced countries, particularly in the major cities, 4G will be available. If it is not, the tablet will look for the next best type, 3G, and if it cannot find that either, it will connect to an EDGE network.

Establishing a Cellular Connection

Before you can get going with cellular, you first need to purchase a service plan – cellular networks are not free. Depending on your carrier and service plan, your tablet may connect automatically to your carrier's fastest available data network. If so, you're good to go.

Alternatively, your carrier may provide you with a SIM card. In this case:

1. Switch the tablet off

2. Insert the SIM card in the tablet's SIM card slot

3. Switch the tablet on

4. It may take a few minutes for your cellular connection to be activated. When it has been, your tablet will automatically begin searching for a network. It will probably find several different types of cellular network and, if so, it will connect to the most recent type

Yet another way is to enter the service plan's configuration details, as supplied by the carrier, in the tablet's network settings:

1. Open the Settings app and then tap 'Wireless & networks'

2. Tap More

3. Tap Cellular networks

4. Enter the configuration details

Managing a Cellular Connection

As we've seen, a cellular connection requires a service plan – and these need to be paid for. To make sure you get value for your money, and also don't get burned by extortionate data roaming charges, it is important to keep on top of this type of connection.

Track Your Data Usage

The big advantage of paying for a cellular data plan is that you will almost always have access to a network regardless of where you are – your email will always work and you will always be able to connect to the Internet.

These data plans are either limited (you can only use a set amount of data, after which you are charged extra) or unlimited (there is no limit to what you can use). If you're on the latter type of plan, you don't have an issue here. If you're using a limited plan though, you most definitely do.

Fortunately, your tablet lets you keep an eye on the amount of data your network connection is using:

1. Open the Settings app and tap 'Wireless & networks'

2. Tap 'Data usage'

3. Here, you'll be able to see precisely how much of your data allowance has been used in specified periods

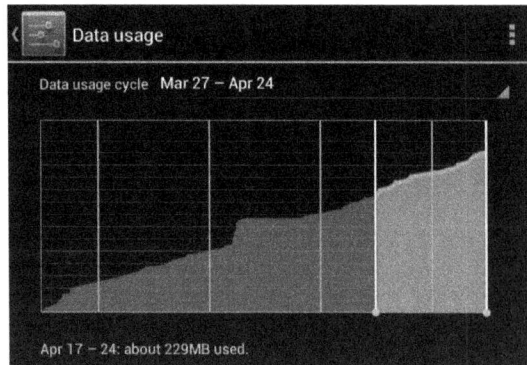

Control Your Data Usage

Your tablet lets you control the amount of data your network connection uses in several ways. One simple method is to just turn data usage off completely; this can be done by tapping the Cellular data switch to Off.

You can also tap the 'Set cellular data limit' switch to On and then specify exactly how much data the network is allowed to use. Be aware that some of the apps on your tablet use your network connection to send and receive data, even when you aren't using them.

All these apps are listed at the bottom of the Data usage window. At the right of each app, you'll see the data it has used. If one is using too much, tap on it and then tap APP SETTINGS. This will allow you to set restrictions on the amount of data the app can use.

Bluetooth Connections

What is Bluetooth?

Bluetooth is a low-power wireless network technology designed for the exchange of data over short distances – typically, 10 meters and less. It is built into literally billions of products: from cars and smartphones to medical devices, computers, headphones, and even toothbrushes.

Bluetooth networks enable the sharing of voice, music, pictures, video and other information wirelessly between paired devices. Typical uses are connecting wireless speakers to playback devices such as smartphones, uploading pictures from cameras, and transferring files from one smartphone to another.

Do not confuse Bluetooth with Wi-Fi – although both are 'wireless', they are not the same at all. For example, Bluetooth networks use virtually no power and, because they don't travel far, are theoretically more secure than Wi-Fi networks that operate over longer distances.

Setting up a Bluetooth connection is a two-stage procedure involving both the tablet and the device being connected to it, as we see below.

Make Your Devices Discoverable

The Bluetooth network is created by a tiny chip built-in to the device that you are connecting wirelessly to your tablet. For it to work, both the device and the tablet need to be made 'discoverable'.

We'll start with your tablet:

1. Open the Settings app

2. In the 'Wireless & networks' section, tap Bluetooth

3. Enable Bluetooth by tapping the switch to the On position – your tablet is now discoverable, or visible

In the Available devices section, you'll see that the tablet is searching for a Bluetooth signal as shown here:

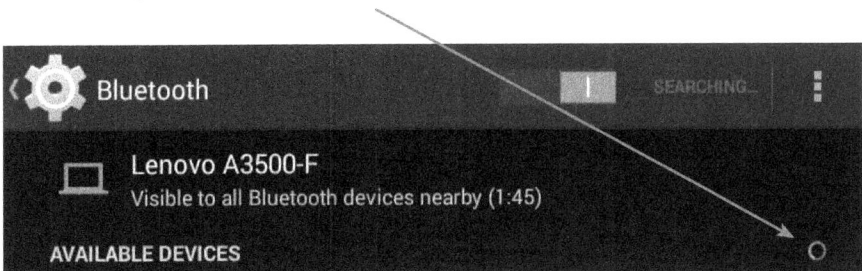

4. Now go to the Bluetooth device

cont'd

5. Switch the device on. If it has a separate switch that makes it discoverable (see the documentation if you are not sure), turn it on. The device will now be discoverable

6. Make sure it is no further than 10 meters or so from the tablet

Pairing Your Devices

Back at the tablet, look in the 'Available devices' section of the Bluetooth settings page. Instead of searching as it was before, you will now see the name of your Bluetooth device (Stuart's iPad in the example below).

The two devices now need to be 'paired', i.e. configured so that they can communicate with each other. To do this:

1. Tap on the Bluetooth device

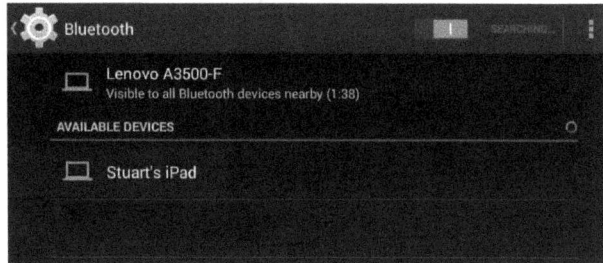

		Bluetooth		SEARCHING...
		Lenovo A3500-F		
		Visible to all Bluetooth devices nearby (1:38)		
AVAILABLE DEVICES				
		Stuart's iPad		

2. Tap Pair in the 'Bluetooth pairing request' window

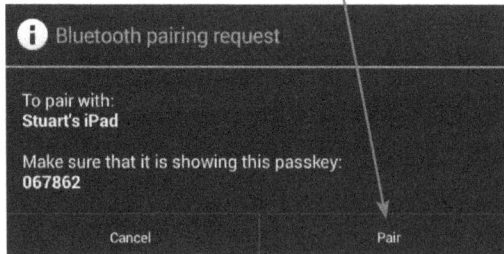

> **ⓘ** Bluetooth pairing request
>
> To pair with:
> **Stuart's iPad**
>
> Make sure that it is showing this passkey:
> **067862**
>
> Cancel   Pair

3. The tablet and the device will now attempt to communicate with each other

4. If the attempt is successful, you will see the device is now listed under Paired devices.

    Note that with some Bluetooth devices a

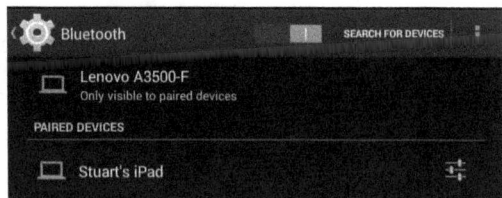

	Bluetooth	SEARCH FOR DEVICES
	Lenovo A3500-F	
	Only visible to paired devices	
PAIRED DEVICES		
	Stuart's iPad	

password will need to be entered during the pairing procedure.

CHAPTER 7

Using the Internet

One of the biggest boons offered by tablets in general is the ability to use the Internet while on the move. Sure, this can also be done on a cell phone but the larger screen of a tablet enhances the experience enormously. In this chapter we show you how to connect your tablet to the Internet.

To use the Internet you will need a web browser and Android provides one of the best – the Chrome app. This offers a good range of features and functions that, quite apart from browsing, also enables you to bookmark your favorite sites, get rid of irritating in-line ads, hide your browsing tracks and much more.

Android Browsers

The Android eco-system belongs to Google and so most Android tablets come with Chrome, Google's web browser, installed as the default browser. Not all do however, and some popular alternatives include: FireFox, Opera, Dolphin, and Maxthon to name just a few.

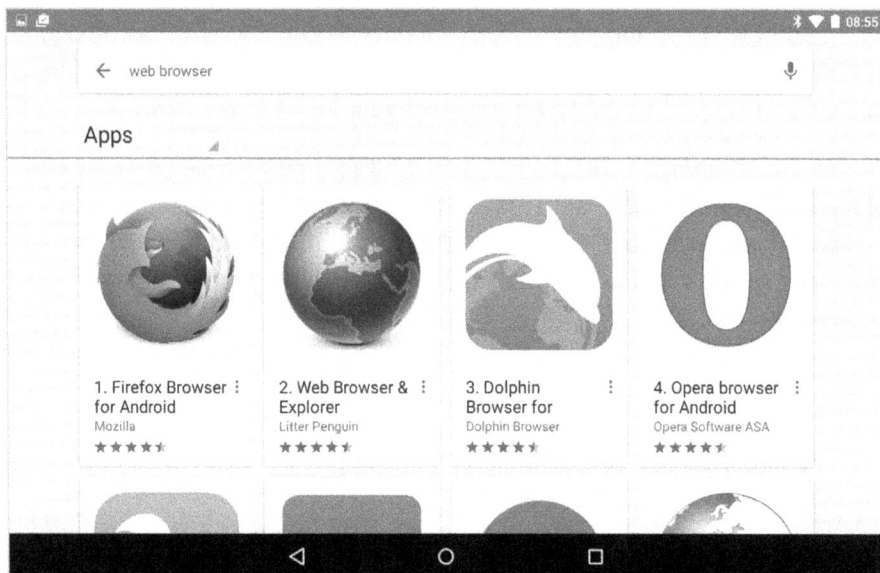

These browsers are available as a free download from the Play Store and while they each have unique features, they all do basically the same thing – allow you to view web pages.

Many of the browsers available in the Play Store are cut-down versions of full-size computer browsers. This has been done in order to make them compatible with tablets and cell phones, which have much lower power and resource requirements. They can display websites in two ways:

- As optimized versions that have been designed and built specifically for viewing on mobile devices

- As full-size versions – the same as you'd see when looking at the sites on a desktop computer or laptop (you will need keen eyesight or a tablet with a large screen to use this option)

Note that you can usually recognize a mobile version of a website by its address – it will have the letter m at the front of the address. For example: **www.m.legalbeagles.com**

The Chrome Web Browser

If you decide to use Chrome as your web browser (and we recommend that you do), it will be as well to familiarize yourself with it beforehand. Tap Chrome on the Apps screen to get started.

The screenshot below shows Chrome's main elements, plus the controls you will use to navigate both the Internet and individual web pages:

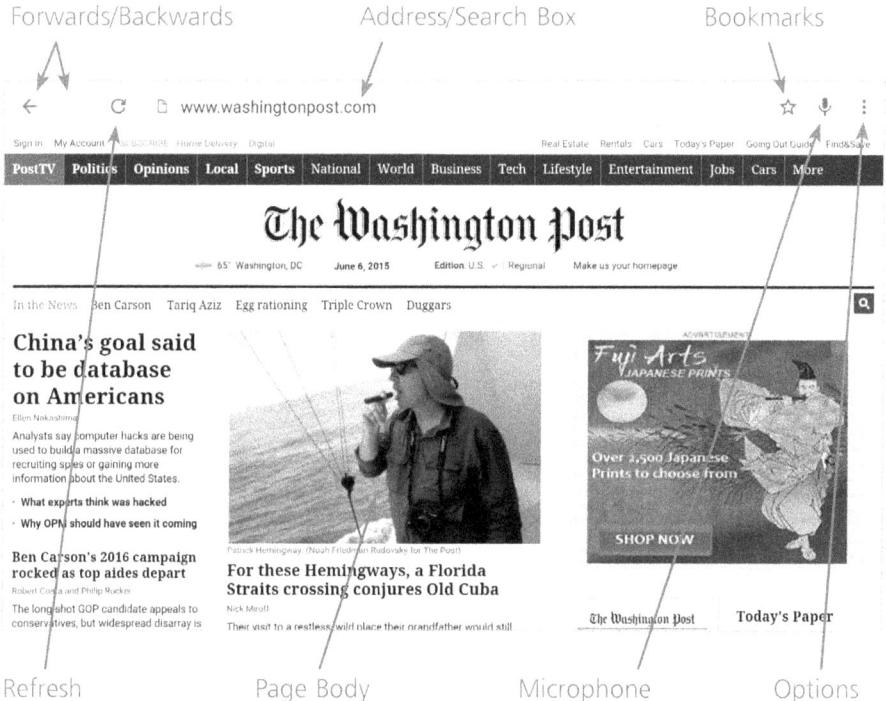

- **Forwards/Backwards** – tap the arrows to navigate between pages

- **Address/Search Box** – this is where you enter the address of a website you want to visit. It also doubles as a search box – simply enter your search term and tap Enter on the keyboard

- **Bookmarks** – this lets you bookmark pages that you may want to visit again

- **Refresh** – the Refresh button lets you reload the page

- **Microphone** – tap this and speak to control the browser with voice commands

- **Options** – these include opening a new tab, looking at your bookmarked pages, viewing your browsing history, printing, and more

Opening a Web Page

To open a web page in Chrome, tap anywhere in the address/search box. The keyboard will open at the bottom of the screen allowing you to type the address.

You'll notice that Chrome tries to predict the address based on what you have already typed in an attempt to speed things up. If it gets it right, stop typing and either tap Enter on the keyboard or tap the prediction. If it gets it wrong, just ignore it and keep typing.

Predicted text (highlighted in blue)

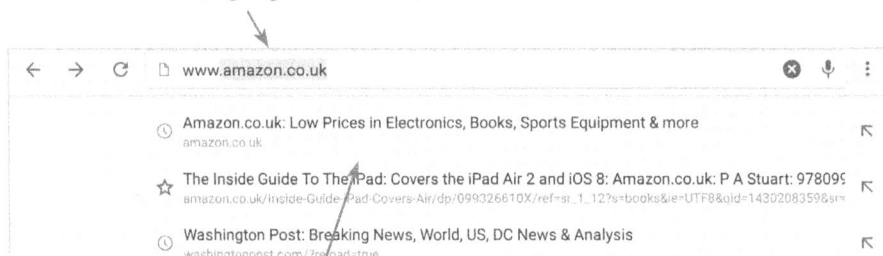

Suggested web pages

Also, as you type, Chrome will suggest pages it thinks are relevant to what you are entering in the address/search box. These appear below the box and are also influenced by pages previously visited and past searches. Just tap one of the links to go to the page.

When you finish a particular browsing session and close Chrome, it will remember the last page visited. The next time you open the browser, it will open that page, the address of which will be in the address/search box as shown below:

To clear the address/search box so you can enter a different address, just tap anywhere in the box. The address will be highlighted as shown above. Clear it by either tapping the X at the right of the address or by simply typing over it.

Viewing & Navigating Web Pages

Viewing and navigating a web page with a touchscreen tablet requires a different technique than the traditional computer/mouse combination. With a tablet, touch gestures are the order of the day and while they are not as precise as a mouse cursor it is, nevertheless, surprising just how effective they are.

● **Panning** – placing a finger on the screen and moving it left, right, up, and down enables you to move, or pan, the page. To move quickly, flick your finger – the faster you flick, the faster the page moves

● **Zooming** – due to the small screen size of tablets, zooming is a much more important issue than it is when browsing the Internet with a full-size computer monitor. Before you do though, try simply rotating the tablet so you are holding it in Landscape mode – this will increase the size of screen elements and may be all that's necessary

If not, double-tap the area you want to zoom into. This may be an area of text, an image, or a form, and it will be magnified to the width of the screen. To zoom back out, double-tap again

To zoom with more control, place two fingers on the screen and move them apart – this action zooms in. Pinching your fingers will zoom out. Note that you should place your fingers on the part of the screen you want to zoom into or out of

● **Move to the top** – if you are down at the bottom of a long page, rather than pan back up, just tap at the top of the screen – this action instantly takes you to the top of the page

● **Links** – web pages often contain links to this, that and the other. If you want to know where a link leads before actually going to it, press and hold the link. A small pop-up will appear and at the top will be the link's address

http://www.amazon.co.uk/Amazon-co-uk-%C2%A310-Gift-Cards-Greeting/dp/B0083U1Y18/ref=sr_1_10?s=gift...

Open in new tab

Open in incognito tab

Copy link address

Copy link text

Save link

Below this, you will see a number of options one of which is 'Open in new tab'. Tap this and the link will open in a new tab – we'll see how to configure this option on the next page.

Another option is 'Copy link address'. Tap this and go to another app, such as Mail or Notes. Position the cursor, tap and then tap Paste. You can now save the link or email it, depending on the app you are using.

Browsing With Tabs

Before the concept of tabbed browsing was conceived, an Internet browsing session could be a somewhat painful experience that involved opening numerous pages, each in its own window, and constant use of the back and forward buttons. Losing your starting point, i.e. the original page, was very easy to do. Also, all these open windows placed a considerable load on the computer's resources that could reduce it to a crawl.

The introduction of tabs resolved these issues and has made it possible to have a number of pages open simultaneously, and to switch between them without ever touching the back and forward buttons. At the same time, the original page can be kept open in case you need to go back.

Opening Tabs
Opening a tab in Chrome is very simple and can be done in two ways:

- At the top-right of Chrome, tap the Options button (see page 79). Then tap 'New tab' at the top of the list of options. All open tabs are shown on the Tab bar, which is situated just above the address/search box, and can be accessed from the bar

Now just type the website address in the tab's address box and press the Enter button

- Links – On page 81 we saw how there are several options with regard to opening web page links, such as Copy and Open. Another of these options is 'Open in New Tab'

Note that when you open a page in a new tab, the current page is kept in the foreground – just tap the new tab to switch to it.

Bookmarks

The Internet is so vast that finding a useful page is a task that can take a long time and involve a lot of searching. So, having found such a page, it makes sense to ensure you can find it again, and quickly, should you ever need to.

This is where bookmarks come in. They allow you to save links to pages you visit often, or might need to access again at some point.

Creating Bookmarks

The procedure for creating a bookmark is very simple as we explain below:

1. In Chrome, open the web page that you want to bookmark

2. Tap on the Star button at the right of the page's address

3. The Add bookmark window opens. The Name and URL fields are already filled in but you can change both if you want to by tapping on them to open the keyboard

4. By default, your bookmarks are saved in a folder called Mobile bookmarks. If you are happy with this, just tap Save at the bottom of the window

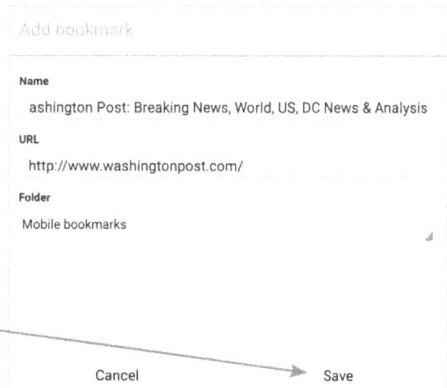

5. If you want to save the bookmark in a different folder, tap on the down-arrow at the right of the Mobile bookmarks text field

6. In the new window, you are offered three folders in which to save your bookmark: Desktop, Other and Mobile. Alternatively, you can tap New folder at the top-right to create your own

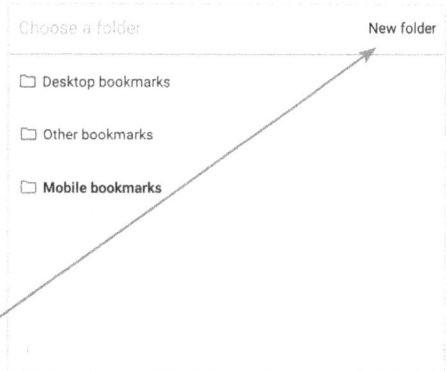

7. In the new Add bookmark window, tap the Save button at the bottom-right to save the bookmarked web page

8. You will now notice that the Star button has turned a darker color. This indicates that the page is bookmarked

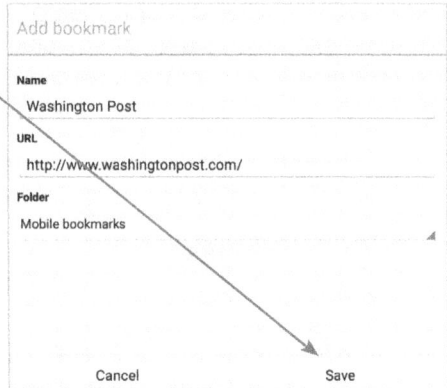

Add bookmark

Name
Washington Post

URL
http://www.washingtonpost.com/

Folder
Mobile bookmarks

Cancel   Save

Viewing Your Bookmarks
To view a page that has been bookmarked:

1. Tap the Options button at the top far-right of Chrome

2. Tap Bookmarks in the Options menu

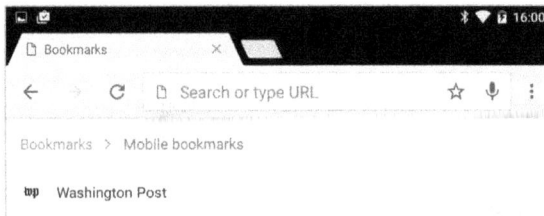

3. From the list, tap the bookmarked page you want to open

Private Browsing

If you are security conscious, you may want to take a look at your tablet's Incognito feature. This allows you to browse the Internet without leaving any traces of what you have been doing.

When in Incognito mode, Chrome doesn't save any website data so there is no way for anyone else to see what you've been up to.

For example:

- Web pages are not stored in Chrome's History list

- Text and images are not stored

- Search box entries are not saved

- AutoFill is disabled

To browse in Incognito mode, open Chrome and tap the Options button at the top-right. From the menu, tap 'New incognito tab'.

New tab

New incognito tab

A new tab opens in Incognito view. Type in the address of the page you want to open.

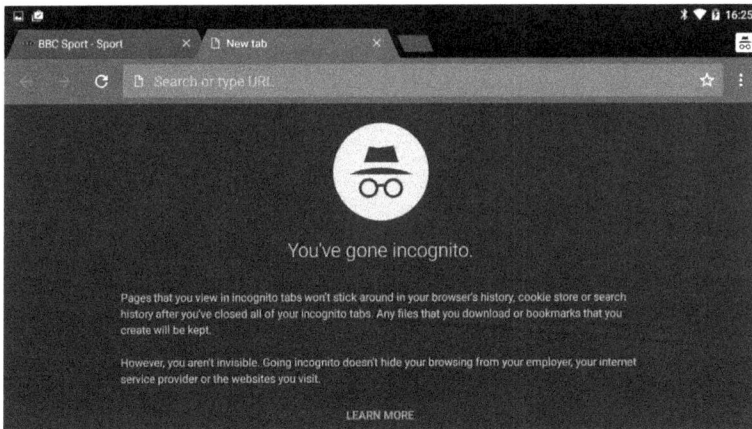

You can always tell when a page is in Incognito mode by the ⚇ icon at the top-right of the browser. If the icon is white, you are in Incognito mode.

You can have both normal and incognito tabs open at the same time – just tap on the icon to switch between them. Whichever view you are in, the tabs in the other view are hidden.

Searching With Chrome

The address box at the top of Chrome doubles as a search box. With it, you can conduct searches not just across the Internet but also on a web page.

Search the Internet

Tap in the box to bring up the keyboard and type in your search term. By default, the search is done via Google and you will see a number of suggestions listed below the search box. If any of these are relevant, tap to open the page.

If not, tap Enter on the keyboard to open a full list of Google search results.

Search a Web Page

Open the page to be searched, and then tap the Options button at the top-right. From the menu, tap 'Find in page' to open a search box. Tap in the box to bring up the keyboard and type in your search term.

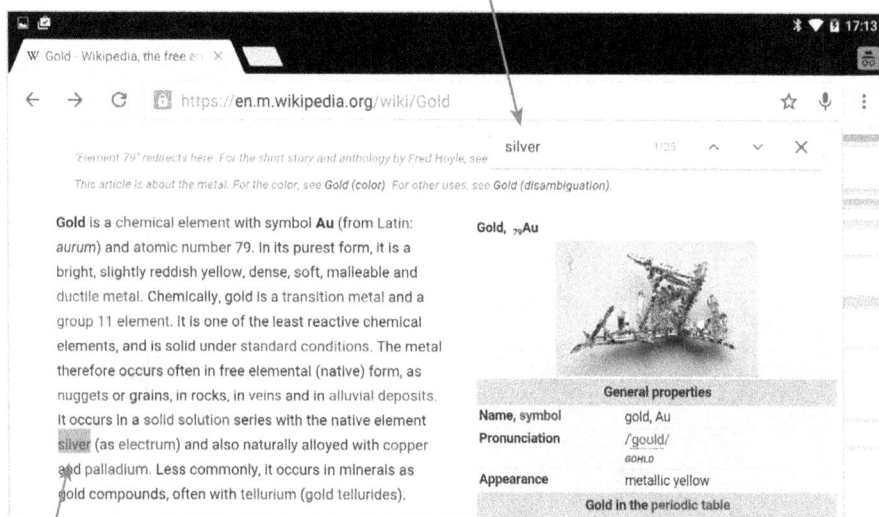

The first instance of the term is highlighted in orange and subsequent instances in yellow. The total number of instances is specified at the right of the search box. To the right of this, you'll see up- and down-arrows that let you move directly from one instance to the next.

You can also search your browsing history. To do this, open the Options menu and tap History. At the top of your History list, you'll see a search box – enter your search term and then tap the Search button on the keyboard.

Desktop View

With the increasing use of smartphones and tablets to browse the Internet, many websites are now offering two versions of their site – a standard desktop view for computers and a mobile view optimized for the small screens found on smartphones and tablets.

When a site is opened in a mobile device, if it offers a mobile view, that is the view the device will load. With mobile views, screen elements are usually stacked one above the other instead of being spread around the pages. As a result, it is not necessary to pan left and right to see all the page's content.

However, while this can be the best way to view the site on a smartphone, it is not necessarily so on a tablet, which has a larger screen. In this case, you may actually prefer to view the site in the desktop view (assuming one is available). You can do this as follows:

1. Tap the Options button at the top-right of the screen

2. Tap 'Request desktop site'

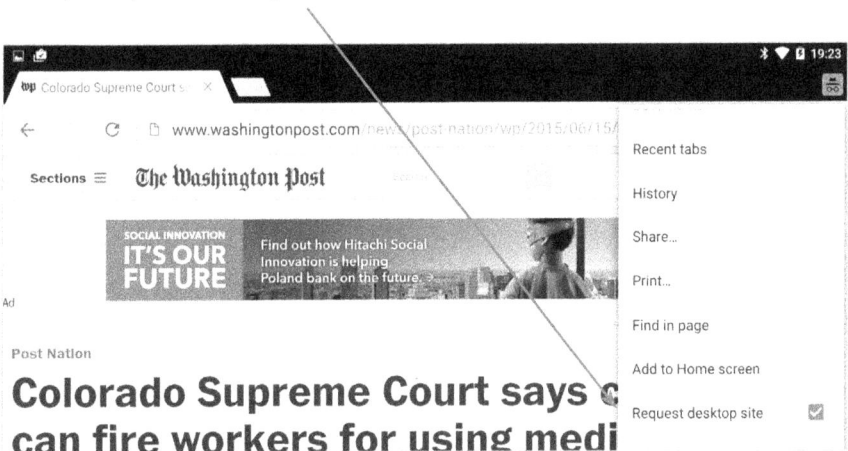

3. If the site offers a desktop view, you will now be switched to it. If it doesn't, nothing will happen – the current view will remain

If a desktop view is available, the site will look just the same on your tablet as it does on a full-size computer screen. Holding the tablet in Landscape mode will increase the size of screen elements but will result in you having to scroll more to see all the content of the various pages.

Note that when you have enabled the Request desktop site option, this will be applied to all subsequent websites that you visit. So if you only want it on the current site, don't forget to disable it when you are finished.

AutoFill

Many sites these days require you to create an account – this will include personal details, such as your home and email addresses, phone number, etc. To log into these accounts, you'll need to enter a password. Then there is online shopping, which of course requires you to enter your credit card details.

To save having to constantly enter this type of information, Chrome provides a feature that can speed things up considerably – it is called AutoFill and it does the work for you by automatically entering the requested information in the various fields.

By default, AutoFill is enabled. However, before you can use it, you will need to specify what information you want it to enter into online forms. To do this:

1. In Chrome, open the Options menu at the top-right and then tap Settings

2. Tap 'Auto-fill forms'

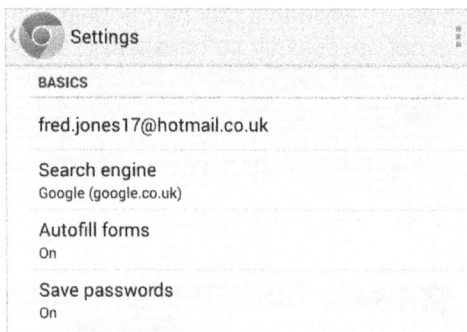

Settings

BASICS

fred.jones17@hotmail.co.uk

Search engine
Google (google.co.uk)

Autofill forms
On

Save passwords
On

3. Tap 'Add profile' to open information fields such as address, phone numbers, and email address. Enter all the info you want the feature to use. You can also add your credit card details

4. By default, AutoFill will save your passwords as you enter them and then subsequently enter them automatically. If you are happy with this, leave the feature enabled. If not, tap the setting and at the top-right, tap the switch to Off

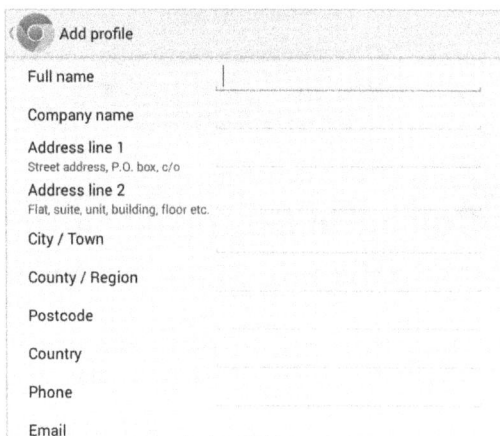

Add profile

Full name

Company name

Address line 1
Street address, P.O. box, c/o

Address line 2
Flat, suite, unit, building, floor etc.

City / Town

County / Region

Postcode

Country

Phone

Email

Note that if you already have a Google account on a different computing device, any of the above information used with that account will be automatically imported to your tablet. If you want to edit any of that information, just tap on it and make your changes.

CHAPTER 8

Staying in Touch

A very important function of your tablet is its ability to let you communicate with the outside world. It offers several methods of doing so, which include email, phone calls, video calls and text messaging.

In this chapter, we take a look at these and see what they have to offer. Email is very popular these days and we explain everything you need to know – the various types of email account, how to set up them up, and how to use your tablet's email app.

Email Services

As with any type of computer, before you can use your tablet for email you must first set up an email account. Your Android tablet provides you with two email apps with which to do this – the Gmail app and the Email app.

You would use the former if you have a Google account, as this also comes with a Gmail account. If you have an existing email account with a different provider, or want to set up a new email account, use the latter.

Types of Email Service

If you decide to use the Email app, when you open it to set up an account as we describe on pages 91-92, you will see that it offers three options: POP3, IMAP and Exchange.

Before we go into the mechanics of setting up an email account, we'll briefly explain the differences between them:

POP3

With POP, emails are stored temporarily on your Internet Service Provider's (ISP's) server. When you connect to the server, the messages are downloaded to your tablet and then deleted from the server.

The advantage of POP is that because all your emails are stored on the tablet, they can be re-read at any time without the need to connect to the Internet. The disadvantage is that they can only be viewed on the tablet to which they were downloaded.

IMAP

IMAP essentially works the other way. Messages are not downloaded to your tablet (although it may seem as though they are). They are actually stored permanently on the ISP's server and you simply read them from there.

The advantage with this method is that your email can be accessed via any device regardless of its location. The disadvantage is that in order to do so, an Internet connection is necessary.

Exchange

Developed by Microsoft, MAPI (Messaging API) is a service that lets applications and email clients communicate with Microsoft Exchange servers – it works on similar principles as IMAP.

Recommended Service

The vast majority of users will be best served by an IMAP email account. The exception would be if you use Hotmail and want to be able to synchronize your email, in which case, we recommend Exchange.

Setting Up an Email Account

The procedure described below is carried out using the Email app:

1. Open the Apps screen and tap the Email app

2. At the opening screen, enter your email address and the password for the email account

3. Tap the Next button. If you are in luck and happen to have the right type of account, it will be recognized and added automatically; if so, skip to Step 7 on the next page. If the account is not recognized, however, tap 'Manual setup'

4. The 'Account type' screen opens as shown below

cont'd

5. Select the type of account you want to set up

6. The 'Incoming server settings' screen opens followed by the 'Outgoing server settings' screen. Enter your connection details (if you don't know what they are, get them from your email provider), and tap Next

Account setup	
Incoming server settings	
Username	stuart.yarnold17@ntlworld.co.uk
Password	••••••••
Server	pop.ntlworld.co.uk
Security type	None
Port	110
Delete email from server	When I delete from Inbox
Previous	Next

Account setup	
Outgoing server settings	
SMTP server	smtp.ntlworld.com
Security type	None
Port	25
☑ Require sign-in	
Username	stuart.yarnold17@ntlworld.com
Password	••••••••

7. The Account settings screen provides you with some configuration options. Select the ones you want to use and tap Next

Account settings	
Account options	
Inbox checking frequency	Every 15 minutes
☑ Notify me when emails arrive	
☑ Sync emails from this account	

8. The final screen confirms that the account has been successfully setup

9. Tap Next to open the Email app and view your downloaded messages

Account setup
Your account is set up and emails are on their way!
Give this account a name (optional)
stuart.yarnold17@ntlworld.com
Your name (displayed on outgoing messages)
stuart.yarnold17
Next

Receiving Email

Once you have set up an email account on your tablet, that account will be the default one for receiving email. However many more accounts you may add subsequently, the first one is the default.

When you want to read your email, go to the Apps screen and tap Email. The app will open in the view shown below:

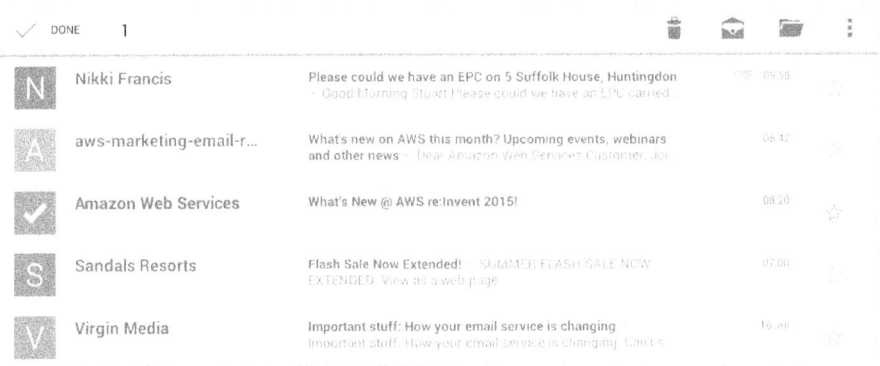

At the left is a list of senders, in the middle is the subject line for each email, and at the right is the time they were received. To read an email, just tap on it and you'll see it open in the message window as shown below (assuming you are holding the tablet in Landscape mode).

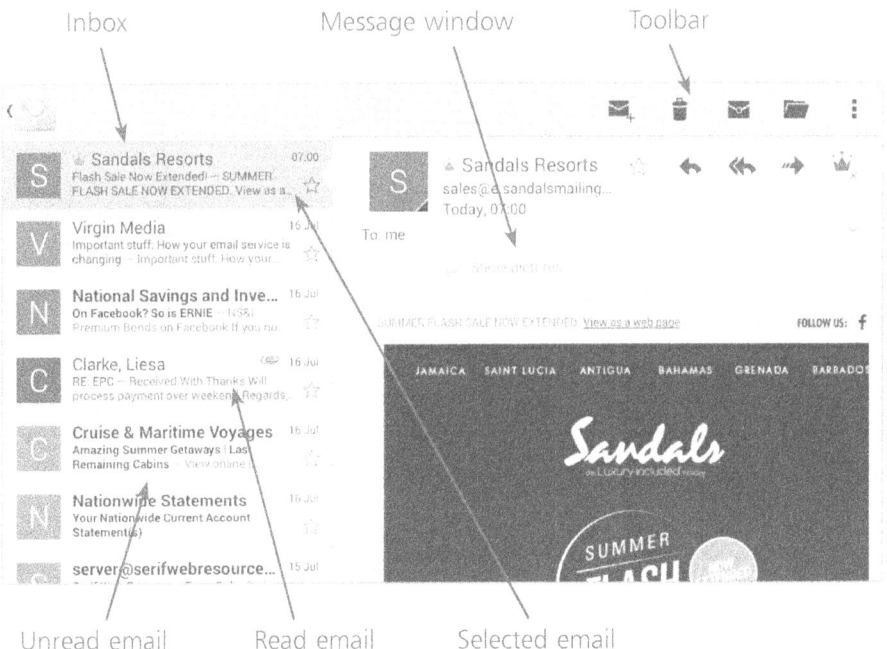

93

cont'd

If you are holding the tablet in Portrait mode, however, the message will open in a full-screen view as we see below:

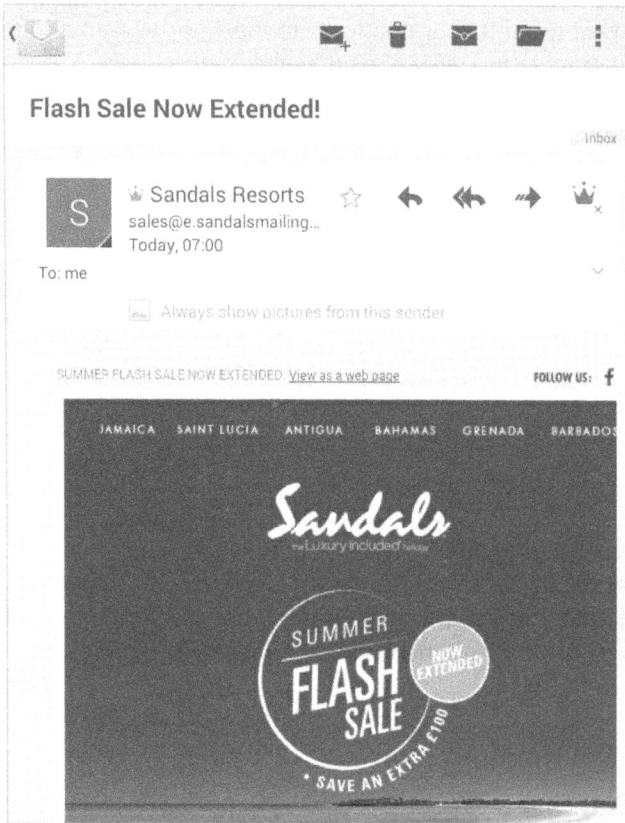

At the top of the screen, you'll see a toolbar with five icons at the right of it. Working from left to right, the first one 📧 is the 'Compose new email' button, which we look at on pages 95-97; the second one 🗑 is the Delete button – just select a message you don't want to keep and hit Delete; the third 📨 is the 'Mark read/unread' button, which will mark emails as either read or unread; the fourth 📁 is the 'Move to' button, which lets you move your messages to specific folders – see page 99 for more on this; and the last ⋮ opens a menu from which you can select Refresh (this manually checks for new emails) and Settings (takes you to the Email app's settings).

The Email app automatically checks for, and downloads, new messages at frequent intervals. You can, however, force a manual check by placing your finger on the first message in the Inbox and swiping down, or by selecting 'Refresh' as mentioned above.

Sending Email

Sending email messages with the Email app is very straightforward. It may not provide some of the features and options found in more complex email clients such as Microsoft Outlook and Mozilla Thunderbird, but the ones it does provide are perfectly adequate as we will see.

Composing an Email Message

To write an email message, tap the 'Compose new email' button at the right of the toolbar. Then:

1. In the To field, start typing the address. As you do so, the Email app displays entries from your contacts list. For example, type J and all contacts beginning with J are shown. Tap to select one or, if it is not in your contacts list, enter the address yourself

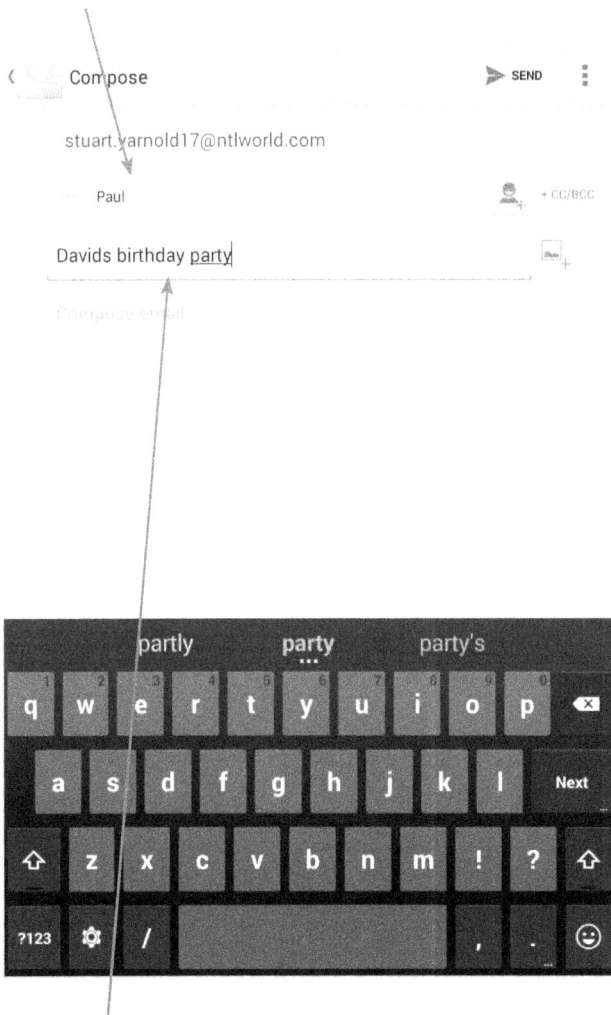

2. Tap in the Subject line and type the subject

cont'd

3. If you have more than one email account set up, you'll see a down-arrow at the right of the From field. Tap the arrow to open a window from where you can select which account the email is being sent from

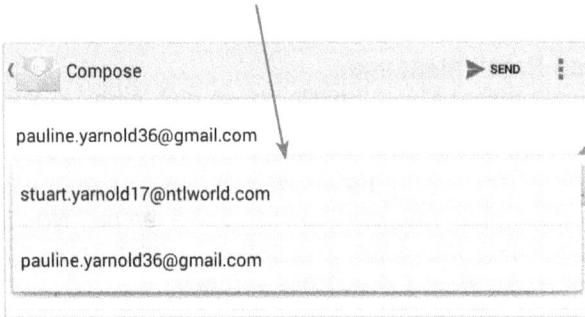

4. Tap in the 'Compose email' field and type your message

5. Note that the Email app does not provide text formatting options such as Bold, Italics and Underline. However, it does you let you Cut, Copy and Paste – press and hold on a word to open blue selection handles as shown below. Drag the handles to select the required text and then select from the options at the top of the toolbar

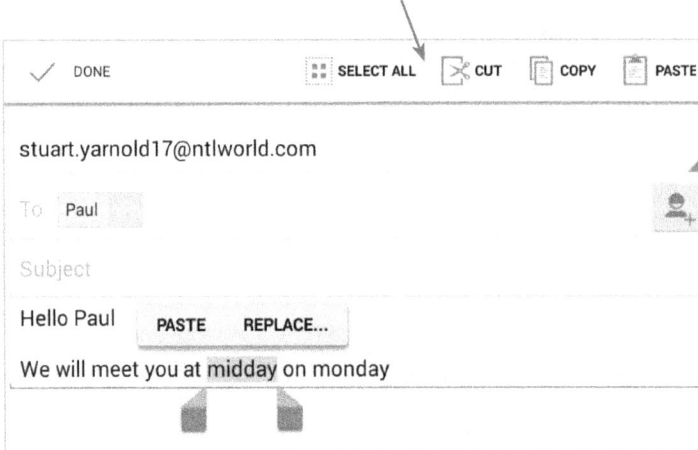

For example, if you want to copy a block of text from somewhere else into your email, select the text from its location as described in step 5, and tap Copy on the toolbar.

Then go to the Email app and tap in the email message window. You'll now see a blinking cursor with a blue handle below. Grab the handle and drag the cursor to the insertion point for the copied text. Then tap Paste

Links

You may want to include a link to a web page in your message. If so, the procedure is as follows:

1. Assuming you are using the Chrome web browser, press and hold on the link – a window will open as shown on the right

   Copy link address

   Save link

2. Tap 'Copy link address'. Next, from Chrome's Options menu at the top-right, tap Share. In the 'Share via' window that opens, tap Email

   Save image

3. An email message window will open with the link pre-pasted into the message. Address it, and add any comments you want to make

Attachments

Before sending your message, you may also want to add an attachment such as a picture. The way to do this is:

1. In the Email app, tap the Attachment button to the right of the toolbar

2. Tap 'Attach file'

3. Browse to and select the file to be attached. It will be inserted into the message

Sending the Message

When you are ready to send the message, tap the Send button which you will find at the right of the toolbar

Your message is sent

Sending message...

Switching Email Accounts

Multiple Accounts

If, like a lot of people, you have more than one email account setup on your tablet, you need a way of quickly switching between them. The way to do this is as follows:

1. Open the Email app

2. Swipe in from the left-hand side of the screen

3. A sidebar will open as shown below:

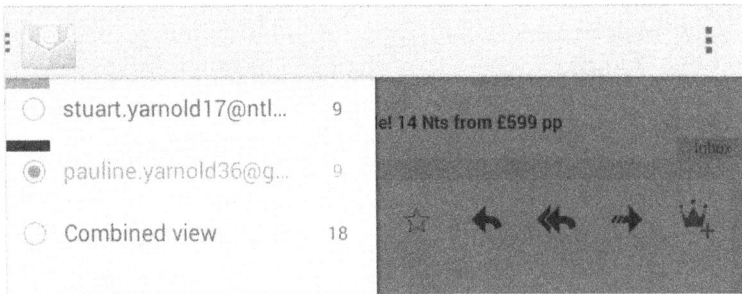

4. At the top of the sidebar, you'll see all the email accounts set up in the Email app (two in the example above)

5. If you tap 'Combined view', received emails from all the accounts will be placed in the inbox

6. At the right of each account is a number that shows the number of unread emails in that account's inbox

Note that while in the combined inbox view, if you should tap the 'Compose email' button to write an email, the account it will be sent from is the default account, i.e. the first account to be set up.

Organizing Your Messages

If you do a lot of emailing, it can be very helpful from an organizational point of view to place your messages in related folders, or mailboxes. To this end, the Email app provides a number of folders that you can use. You can see those folders by opening the Email app and accessing the sidebar as explained above.

Below the accounts, you will see a list of the default email folders. Note that you cannot create folders yourself – you can only use the ones provided.

cont'd

To organize your messages with the default folders, do the following:

1. Open the email to be moved

2. Tap the 'Move to' button on the toolbar at the top. A window showing the default folders opens as shown below:

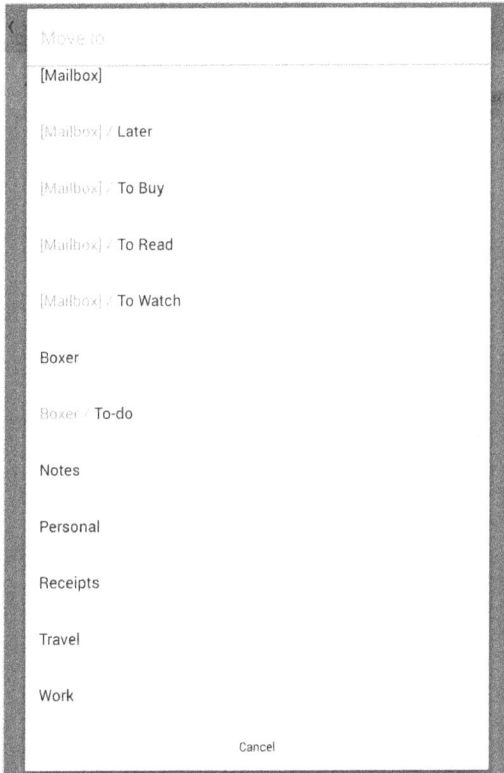

3. Select the folder you want to copy the message to by tapping on it. Then tap OK. Now go to the folder and you'll see the message there

Deleting Messages
To remove a message from any folder, place your finger at the right of the message and swipe to the left. You'll see the message below telling you it has been deleted. If you change your mind at the last minute, tap UNDO

Email Settings

The Email app provides a number of settings that you can use to set up the app to suit your way of working. To access the settings:

1. Open the Email app and tap the ⦂ button on the toolbar

2. Tap Settings to access the Settings screen. Tap on General settings to access generic email settings, or tap an account to access settings specific to that account

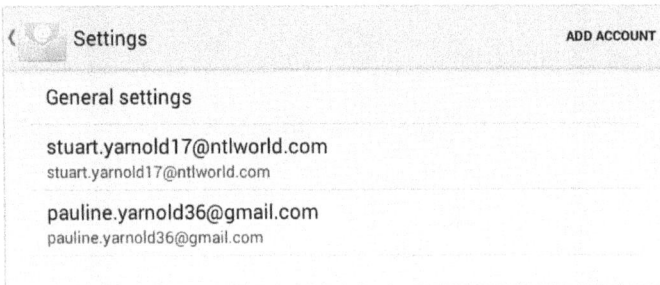

General settings include:

Confirm before deleting/sending – off by default, enabling these two settings will cause a confirmation window to open asking if you want to send or delete a message

Auto-advance – whenever you open an email in your inbox and then archive or delete it, you're taken back to your inbox. By enabling 'Auto-advance' you will, instead, be taken automatically to the next conversation

Swipe to delete – this option lets you delete a message by swiping it from right to left

Reply all – when there are multiple recipients of a message and you want to respond to all of them, tap 'Reply to all' below the message. Enabling 'Reply to all' makes it the default action

Specific account settings include:

Signature – A signature is a bit of text (such as your contact information or a favorite quote) that's automatically inserted at the bottom of every message you send This setting lets you specify a signature

Notifications – by default, a notification pops up on the screen whenever an email arrives. If you want to, you can turn this off here

Sync frequency – this setting lets you specify how often the Email app checks for new messages

Phone Calls

A recent development in the world of Android is free, or reduced rate, phone calls. These can be made via Wi-Fi or data connections such as 3G and 4G. To do it, you use the Hangouts app. Before you can do so though, you must download the Hangouts dialer from the Play Store. Having done so, do the following:

1. On the Apps screen, tap Hangouts

2. Sign in to your Google account, or create one

3. Tap Open

4. Tap the dial pad button to open the dial pad

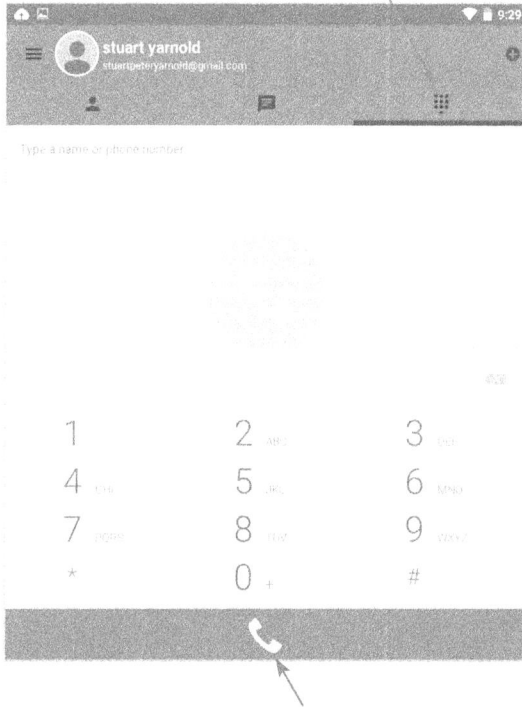

Enter the number and then tap the phone button to initiate the call – that's all there is to it.

Hangouts calls are free when you call other Hangouts users and when you call the US or Canada. A few US and Canadian destinations will cost USD 0.01 per minute depending on the specific phone number.

About the only proviso to making phone calls with Hangouts is that you will need to have a Google account (if you haven't, you will be prompted to open one during the Hangouts setup procedure).

Video Calls

You can also make video calls with your tablet. While it is possible to do this with the Hangouts app, a simpler method is to use Skype – a free app available from the Play Store:

Locate and download the app as described on pages 62-63 & 65.

One proviso with Skype is that you can only connect to other Skype users. With that in mind, initiate a Skype call as follows:

1. Open the app from the Home screen

2. If you already have a Skype account, sign in to it. If not, you are prompted to open one

3. Once signed in, you are taken to the main screen

4. Tap the blue arrow at the right of 'People'

5. Tap the button at the far-right of the toolbar and then tap 'Add people'

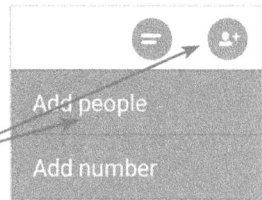

6. In the 'Find people on Skype' box, type the name of the person you want to contact. When you have found the name, tap it

7. In the next screen, tap 'Add to contacts'. The person will now be sent a Skype request, which they will have to accept before you can make a call to them. Once they have, their name will be added to your Skype contacts list

8. Now go back to the main screen. Under People, you will see your contacts. All the contacts you add to Skype are listed here. To make a call to one, tap on the person's name

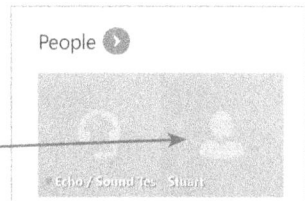

9. In the new screen, on the toolbar at the top, tap the phone button to place a voice call to the contact

10. Tap on the video button if you want to make a video call to the contact

Text Messaging

A very popular use of tablets is keeping in touch by text messages. With Android, this function is provided by the Hangouts app we looked at on page 101. Note that you will only be able to communicate by text messaging with people who have Google accounts.

Do it as follows:

1. Open Hangouts from the Apps screen

2. Tap the People button at the left of the toolbar

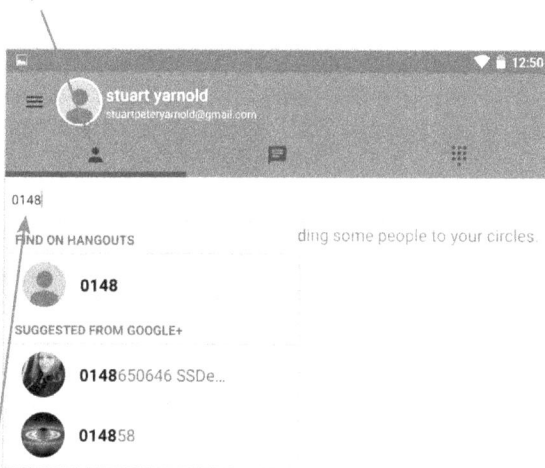

3. In the box just under the toolbar, type the person's name, phone number or email address

4. When you see the required person in the list of contacts that opens below, tap to select him or her

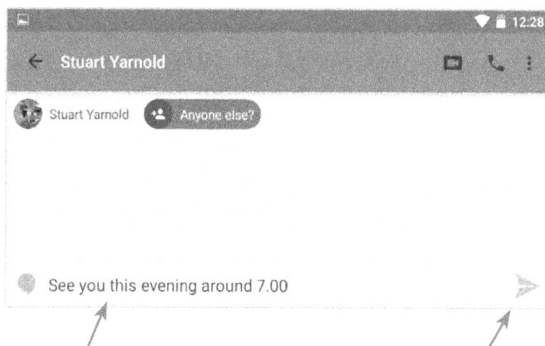

5. Type your message in the box and then tap the Send button

Social Networking

Social networking on Android tablets is provided by Google+, which can be accessed on the Apps screen. The main page (shown below) provides a continuously updated stream of conversations and shared content.

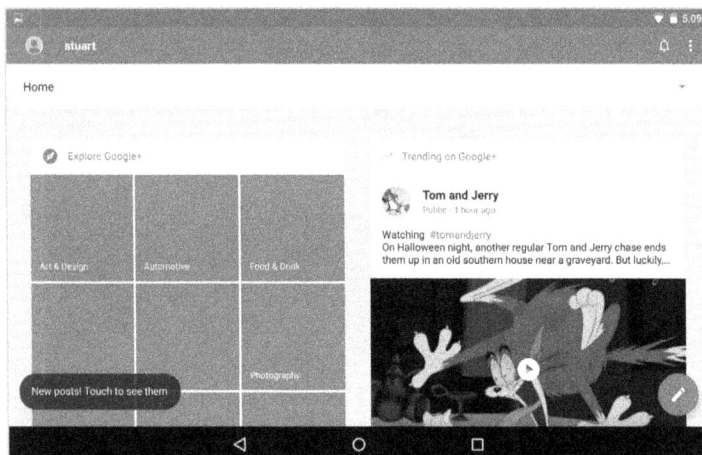

- When you add a contact to your Google+ account, you assign them to one or more 'circles' – a way of categorizing and organizing people. When you first sign up, you'll see some circles that have already been set up by Google, including 'Friends' and 'Acquaintances'

- You can share messages or links with everyone or just with those within designated circles. This gives you more flexibility than Twitter and is a similar concept to Groups on Facebook

- Your circles are private – no one can see how you've named your circles or which circles they or anyone else have been put in

- The Notifications section lets you know when someone adds you to one of their circles (though not which circle), and when someone has commented on or reacted to content that you've shared or commented on yourself

- You can make comments underneath content shared by other users that you follow, and you can also +1 it. The latter is similar to Facebook's Liking feature

- You can also share that content if the original poster allows it – this is similar to retweeting on Twitter

- If the original poster allows it, after you interact with a post Google+ threads responses and informs you of any updates

CHAPTER 9

Organizing Your Life

In Chapter 9, we see how your tablet can be gainfully employed in helping to organize your life. This is done with the aid of three apps supplied with the device – People, Calendar, and Keep, plus an app called RemindMe that is available from the Play Store. Of these, People and Calendar are the most useful and will make it easy to stay in touch with the people and events in your life.

The RemindMe and Keep apps help you to remember all the little things that need attention during your day. We also take a look at your tablet's Priority Mode feature and see what can done with it.

Contacts

These days people have a lot of stuff to remember – cell phone and landline numbers, not to mention home, website and email addresses. To help do it, all tablets and smartphones provides an electronic version of the traditional address book – the Contacts list. The version supplied with Android is the People app.

The People app serves another purpose as well – many of the other apps on your tablet use the information on it – this helps to speed up operations and generally make life simpler and easier for you, the user. Email apps are a typical example of this.

Therefore, if you want to make the best use of the functions provided by your tablet, it is important to ensure that the information in your People app is up-to-date and as comprehensive as possible – this applies particularly to your own personal contact.

Creating Contacts

To create your personal contact details and those of your friends and family:

1. Open the Apps screen and tap People

2. In the first screen, tap the New Contact 👤 button at the top-right. The 'Add new contact' screen opens as shown below

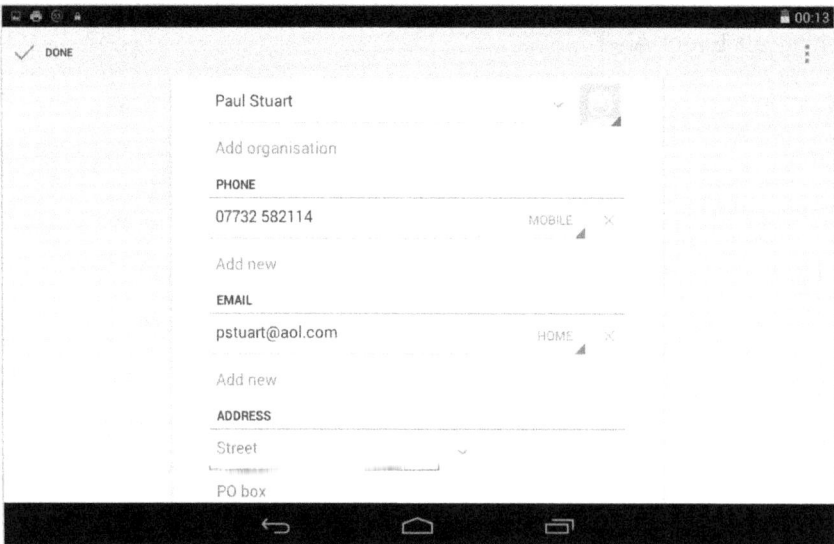

3. Work down the screen filling in the information fields as necessary

cont'd

4. To the right of several of the fields, you'll see a down-arrow – tap the arrow to reveal more fields

5. You can associate a picture with the contact by tapping the button at the right of the name field and then either choosing a photo from the Gallery app, or taking one with the camera

6. When you've finished, tap Done at the top-left of the screen

The next time you open the People app, you'll see the contact, plus any others you may have added, listed on the opening screen as shown below:

You'll also see at the top 'Set up my profile'. This is for you to use in setting up your own personal contact. Tap the 'Set up my profile' link and enter your own details just as you would for any other contact.

Note: if you entered your personal details such as name, email address, etc, during the tablet's initial setting up procedure, your personal contact will have been created automatically. You can however, edit it if necessary by tapping the pencil icon at the top-right.

Whichever, once created your personal contact is always displayed at the top of the contact list.

Groups
A useful organization feature of the People app is Groups. Open a contact and you'll see a Groups link at the right. Tap the down-arrow at the right of it and then tap 'Create new group' to create one.

The contact is automatically assigned to the group. Once a group has been created, other contacts can also be assigned to it. In this way, you can organize your contacts in a logical manner – a Work group for your work contacts, a Family group for family members, and so on.

Using Contacts

To use your contacts list, open the People app. At the opening screen, you'll see all your contacts listed. To open one, just tap on it.

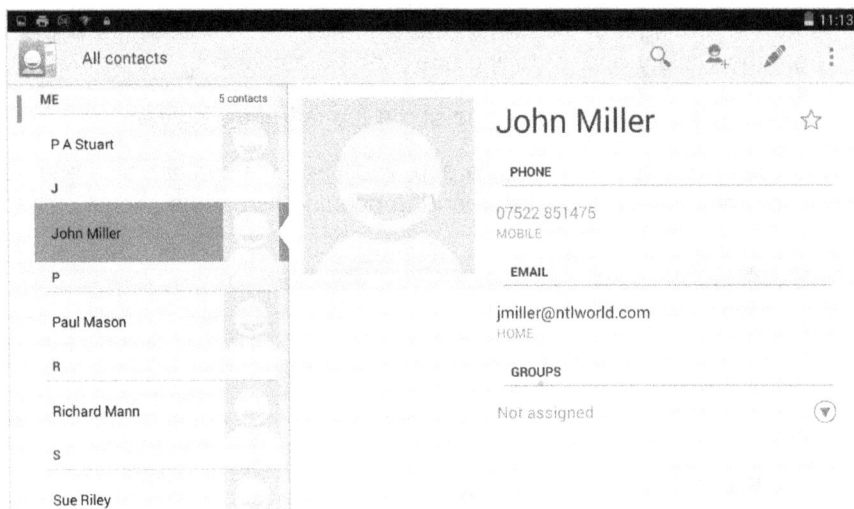

Individual contact screens as shown above offer several options. These include:

- Tap the Star icon at the top-right of the contact's picture to add the contact to your list of Favorite contacts. Access these by tapping All Contacts at the top-left of the screen

- Tap the pencil icon to edit the contact's details

- Tap the three-dot icon at the far-right to access a number of options that include deleting or sharing the contact, placing it on the Home screen where it will be quickly accessible, and the app's settings

- To the right (or below) the picture, depending on the tablet's orientation, you will see the contact's main details – phone numbers, home address, website address, etc

- To send an email to the contact, just tap on the email field – a new email message window will open with the contact's address already filled in. Just add your text and tap Send

- If the contact has a website, tap the address and Chrome will spring to life and open the site. Tap on a house address and the Maps app will open a map showing the exact location of the address

The Android Calendar

People live busy lives – they have places to go, people to see. The busier they are, the more things they have to remember and this is where the electronic calendar comes into play.

Supplied with your tablet is an extremely useful calendar app that will ensure you never again forget a birthday, business appointment, lunch date, or anniversary. The app remembers all these dates and times and can also prompt you with reminders just to make sure you don't forget.

On the Apps screen, tap Calendar:

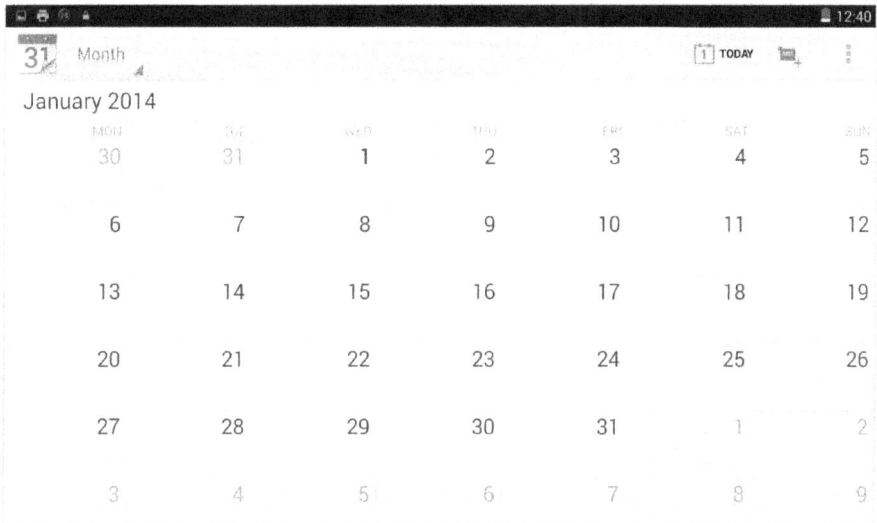

The calendar app offers four views and opens at the one last in use. These are Day, Week, Month and Agenda, and can be selected from the Options menu at the top-right of the screen.

- **Day** – in this view, you see the events for the selected day. A timeline and list of events is displayed on the left

- **Week** – this view shows all the events in any given week and the times they are scheduled for – you may have to scroll down to see them all

- **Month** – in the Month view, you see all the events in any given month, and the days they have been scheduled for

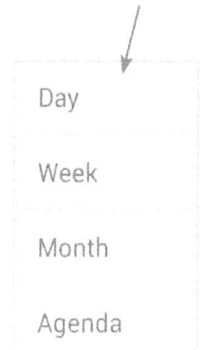

- **Agenda** – Agenda gives you two views: on the left, you see all the events on the calendar listed in order and, on the right, the details of the events as shown below:

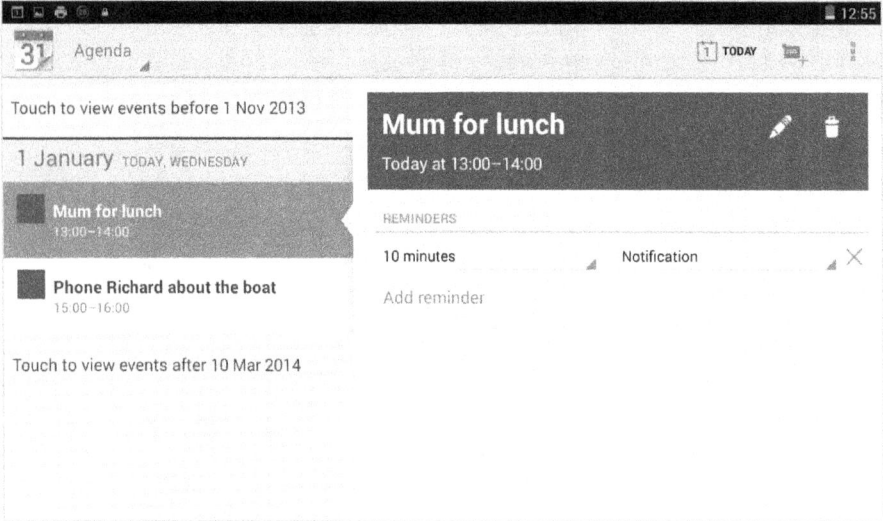

With busy calendars that have lots of events, you will have to scroll down to see them all.

If you need to edit an event for any reason, tap the pencil icon at the right of the event's heading to open the 'Edit event' screen. Make your changes and tap the Save button.

To delete an event, open the Edit screen and tap Delete at the bottom.

Adding a Calendar Event

An 'event' is calendar-speak for an entry. To add an event to your calendar, follow the steps outlined below:

1. Open the Day, Week or Month view and tap the + button at the top-right

2. The 'New event' screen opens as shown here

3. In the What field, enter a name for the event

4. The Where option lets you specify the location of the event (assuming there is one)

5. Set the day and time the event begins and ends using the From and To options

6. If the event is an all day one, check the All day box

7. You can add anyone who has an email address to your event by tapping in the Guests field. Start typing the name of the person and choose a result from your contacts. You can also type an email address to invite people who aren't in your contacts list. When you save your event, an email invitation will be automatically sent to the people you have invited

8. Enter a description of the event in the Description field

9. In the case of a recurring event, tap the down-arrow at the right of the Repetition field and set the required day and frequency

10. If you want to be alerted to the event, tap Add reminder – we look at this option in more detail on the next page

11. If you don't want to be disturbed by others, set the 'Show me as' field to Busy. Otherwise, choose Available

12. In the Privacy field, selecting Default or Private means you are only person who will be able to see the event

13. Tap Done at the top-right of the screen when you are finished

Setting an Event Alert

If you're the type of person who tends to forget things, one of the most useful features of electronic calendars may provide the answer. We're talking here about the Calendar app's Reminders feature, which will let you know about an upcoming event a set period beforehand.

Setting an Alert

To ensure you don't forget a birthday or whatever:

1. Open the calendar and go to the date that contains the event

2. Tap the event and the event's details window opens

3. Tap Reminders

4. A pop-up window will open showing a number of options that range from 0 minutes all the way up to 1 week as shown on the right. Just tap the one required

5. Tap Done at the top-right of the screen to save the alert

Should you feel the need, you can also set a backup alert in case the first one doesn't get your attention.

To do this, just repeat the above procedure by tapping the Add reminder link that appears below the first one.

You can actually add up to five alerts in this way.

When the alert activates, the Calendar app will automatically display it on the screen. Just to make sure you get the message, your tablet will also emit a beep.

10 minutes
15 minutes
20 minutes
25 minutes
30 minutes
45 minutes
1 hour
2 hours
3 hours
12 hours
24 hours
2 days

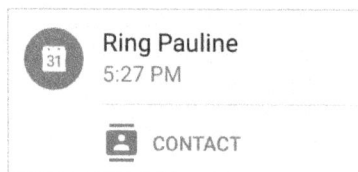

Ring Pauline
5:27 PM

CONTACT

Reminders

The Calendar app is excellent for tracking appointments, meetings, etc. You can also make sure you don't forget the appointment or meeting by setting an alert as we have just seen.

But what about the multitude of daily tasks that need to be done at specific times but do not really warrant a calendar entry and alert? Examples include taking the cake out of the oven, watching a program on the TV, calling someone, etc.

The solution is a Reminders app. Android tablets do not usually provide an app of this type so to get one you will probably need to pay a visit to the Play Store. Here, you will find a multitude of them.

One that we recommend is called RemindMe – just type this into the Play Store's search box and you'll see it – download the app as previously explained. Then proceed as follows:

Setting a Reminder
To set up a reminder with RemindMe, tap the RemindMe app on the Home screen to open it. Then:

1.   Tap New Reminder

2.   Tap Set Timer and in the screen that opens drag the sliders to set a countdown before the reminder is activated

3.   Alternatively, to set a specific day and time, tap the calendar and clock buttons

4.   Enter a descriptive name for the reminder in the Description box

5.   Tap Set Reminder

6.   A new screen will open showing all pending reminders

It is also possible to set recurring reminders with the app. In this case, instead of tapping New Reminder in Step 1, press and hold until the new screen opens. You'll see an option that lets you specify the period before the reminder is issued again – Daily. Weekly, Monthly or Custom.

Note: Remindme is designed for use with smartphones. However, it works perfectly well on tablets.

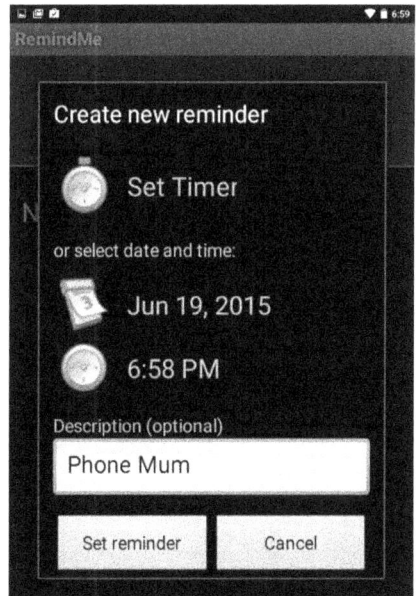

Managing Reminders

When the RemindMe app issues a reminder, your tablet will play a note and a message will briefly flash up on the screen:

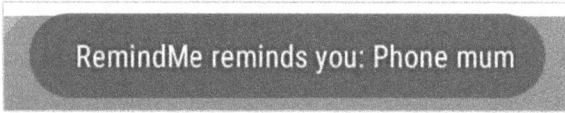

RemindMe reminds you: Phone mum

You then need to acknowledge receipt of the alert in order to remove it. To do this, open the tablet's Notifications by swiping down from the top of the screen – you'll see a notification advising the alert has been issued. Tap the notification and you will be taken to the RemindMe app's Pending screen from where you can delete the alert.

Configuring the RemindMe App

Configuration options for the RemindMe app can be accessed by tapping the █ button at the bottom-right of the screen, and then tapping Settings:

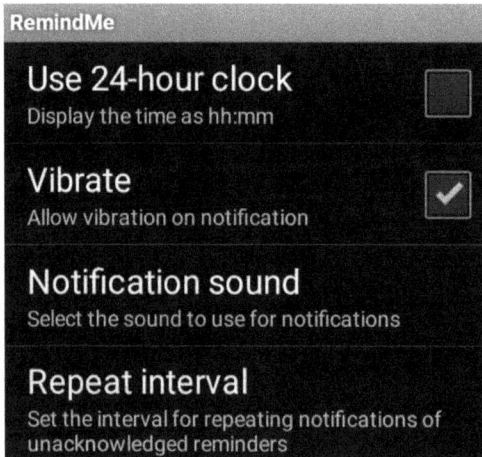

RemindMe

Use 24-hour clock
Display the time as hh:mm

Vibrate
Allow vibration on notification

Notification sound
Select the sound to use for notifications

Repeat interval
Set the interval for repeating notifications of unacknowledged reminders

They include:

● Using a 24-hour clock

● Enabling or disabling tablet vibration on receipt of an alert

● Specifying the sound to be used for notifications

● Specifying the interval at which unacknowledged reminders are repeated

Notes

When it comes to making notes on your tablet, Android supplies the Keep app – this allows you to quickly jot down notes as and when they come to mind. However, it is not installed on your tablet by default – you will have to download it from the Play Store.

Note that the installation will also involve downloading and installing an update to Google Play Services and then signing in to your Google account. Once done, open the app by tapping Keep on the Apps screen:

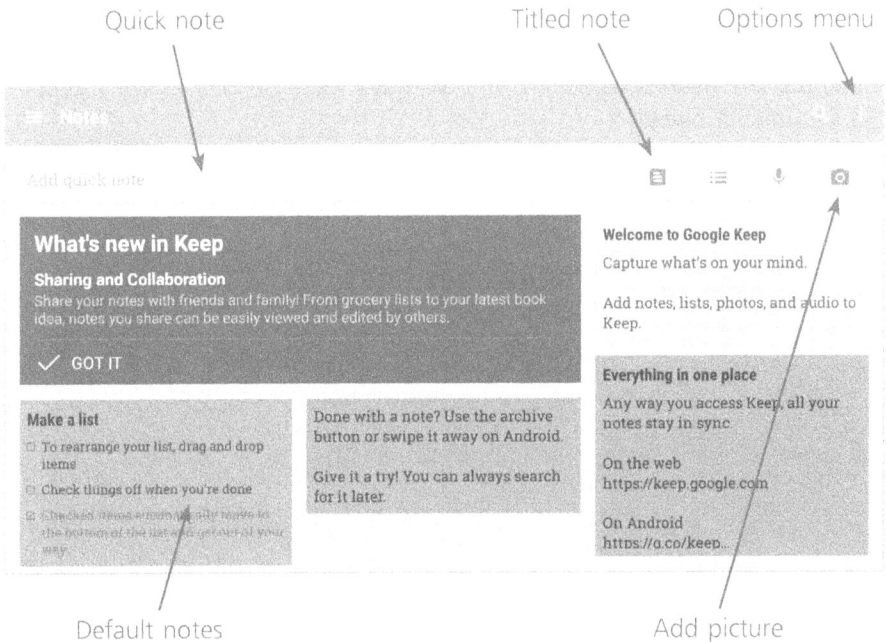

Quick note   Titled note   Options menu

What's new in Keep

Sharing and Collaboration
Share your notes with friends and family! From grocery lists to your latest book idea, notes you share can be easily viewed and edited by others.

✓ GOT IT

Make a list
☐ To rearrange your list, drag and drop items
☐ Check things off when you're done
☑ Checked items automatically move to the bottom of the list and get out of your way

Done with a note? Use the archive button or swipe it away on Android.

Give it a try! You can always search for it later.

Welcome to Google Keep
Capture what's on your mind.

Add notes, lists, photos, and audio to Keep.

Everything in one place
Any way you access Keep, all your notes stay in sync.

On the web
https://keep.google.com

On Android
https://g.co/keep...

Default notes   Add picture

Keep opens in the above view. The first thing you'll notice is a number of differently colored default notes in the lower part of the screen – What's new in Keep, Welcome to Google Keep, Make a list, etc. To read any of these, tap on the note to open it in a full-screen view. Having done so, you can then delete the note by tapping the Options menu button at the top-right and tapping Delete note.

You can also remove them by simply swiping them off the screen. Note that this doesn't delete the note; it moves it to an archive folder from where it can be restored if necessary.

Another option available from the Options menu is 'Single-column view'. Selecting this stacks your notes in a vertical list with the most recent placed at the top. This makes it easier to read and manage your notes, and we recommend that you choose this option.

Creating Notes

The Keep app provides you with two options when you want to make a note – a quick basic note or a titled note. Select the former by tapping in the 'Add quick note' box at the top of the screen and typing in your note.

If you tap the Titled note button, you will have more options as we see in the screenshot below:

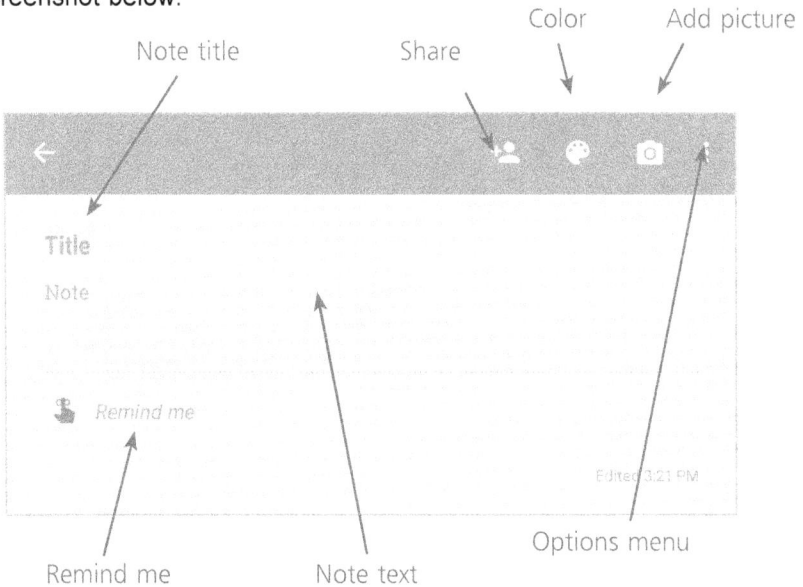

- Tap the Title box and type a title for your note – this will appear in Bold

- The Share button lets you specify someone's email address so the note can be shared with them

- Tap the Color button and you will be able to choose from eight colors for the background color of the note

- The Add picture button gives you two options: take a picture with the tablet's camera or browse to and select one already on the tablet

- 'Remind me' lets you set an alert for the note, by either time or location

- Type the text for your note in the Note box

116

To-Do Lists

A function related to notes is to-do lists – a grocery shopping list is a typical example. The Keep app has this covered as well.

Open the app and, from the toolbar at the top, tap the List button. An empty to-do list opens. Start by typing a title if you want one by tapping in the Title box. Then tap on the + sign and type a list item. As you type, you'll notice a checkbox appear at the left of each item:

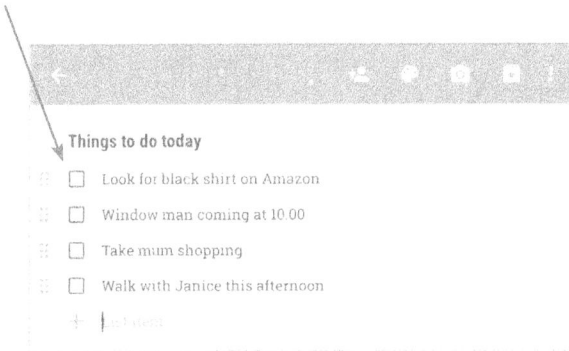

When you've finished the list, you'll see it at the top of the main screen

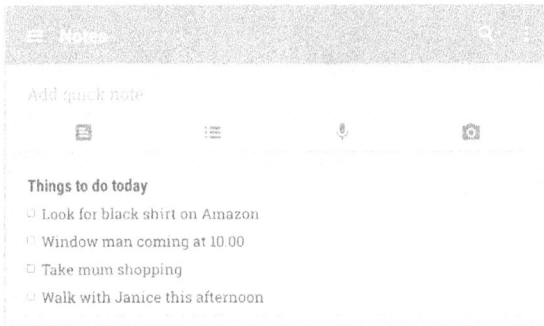

As you work through the list, you can cross off items by tapping in the associated checkboxes

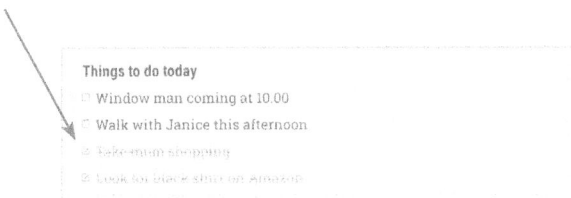

If you don't want the checkbox feature, it can be turned off in the Options menu at the top-right of the screen

Do Not Disturb

While your tablet may be an excellent device for communication purposes and providing audio notifications, there will inevitably be times when you simply do not want to hear from it – a business meeting for example. If so, you need a way of silencing the device.

The types of sound you may need to mute are phone calls (assuming you have a cellular model), calendar alerts, and app notifications.

Phone calls

Neither Android KitKat or Jelly Bean provide a default app for blocking phone calls. Therefore, you need to head off to the Play Store and see what's available there. One that we recommend is called 'Do Not Disturb' by Cabooze Software.

This app is designed for use with smartphones but works equally well on tablets, letting you silence phone calls on cellular models and audible reminders from the Calendar app.

When you run the app for the first time, it opens in the following view:

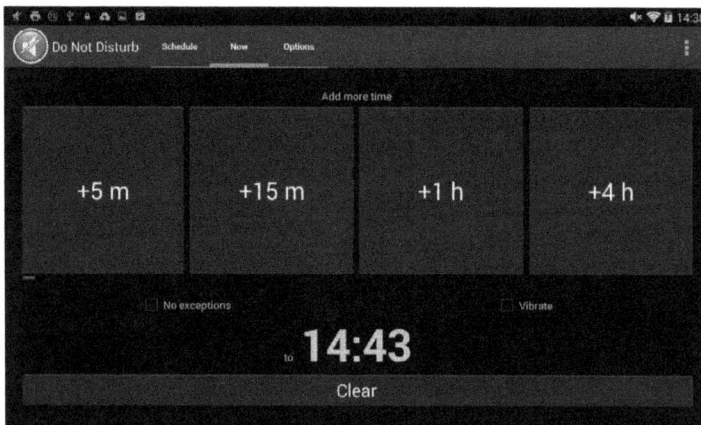

To block all phone calls, just tap one of the four time options. For example, tap +5m to mute the tablet for five minutes. Tap it again to add another five minutes. The time the tablet is muted to is displayed below – 14:43 in our example above.

Below the time options are two settings: No exceptions and Vibrate. They both mean exactly what they say – tapping No exceptions means the tablet will be silent regardless of what exceptions have been set in the schedule.

If you need more specific settings, tap Schedule at the top of the screen. In the window that opens, you will see an Auto Mute option that gives you two pre-configured muting schedules.

cont'd

To activate these, tap the switch at the top-right to On.

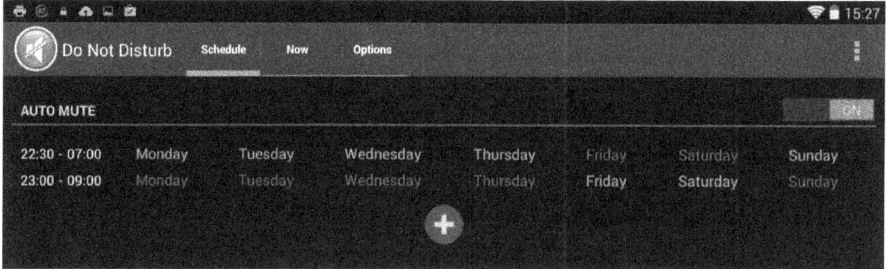

To alter the settings on one of the pre-configured schedules to your own requirements, tap the schedule. Alternatively, tapping the + button below lets you create a schedule of your own. In either case, a pop-up window will open that lets you configure the date and time settings.

Calendar Alerts

Settings for muting audible calendar alerts are in the Calendars section of the Schedule screen.

Tapping the 'Follow a calendar' option will mute any alerts that may occur during the selected calendar's events.

For more options, tap 'Calendar rules'. This provides a number of settings such as which calendars to track. You can also specify by how many minutes to defer the calendar mute; both early and late.

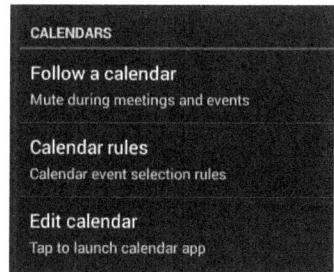

App Notifications

To silence the various notifications made by the apps on your tablet, you have two ways to go:

The first is to silence them all. Do this by opening the Settings app and then tapping 'Audio profiles' in the Device section. To silence the tablet completely, select either Silent or Meeting.

The second is to silence specific apps. To do this, open the app and take a look in its settings – there may be an option that lets you silence it. If not, open the Settings app and tap Apps in the Device section. In the window that opens, swipe to the right until you see the All section – this shows all the apps on the tablet. Find the one you want to silence and tap on it.

Silence the app by unchecking the 'Show notification' checkbox.

119

Useful Organization Apps

The organization apps supplied with Android tablets are not usually the best examples of their type. You will find better ones, not to mention a much greater selection, in the Play Store. Some well known apps are:

Evernote
Used by millions of people all over the world, Evernote is probably the most popular of all the note-taking apps. It offers a text editor, photo upload tool, and voice recording, plus some excellent tools that make it a snap to organize, find and edit your notes.

Also, all your notes are saved in the Cloud – this means they can be accessed from any device and from any location, as long as an Internet connection is available.

OneNote
From the maker of the Windows operating system, Microsoft, OneNote is another well regarded note-taking app. As with Evernote, all the notes you create are saved in the Cloud and can thus be accessed on other devices.

Features include the ability to make annotations, tagging, and password protection. It is also completely free, unlike Evernote where it is necessary to pay for a premium account in order to access all its features.

Dropbox
Dropbox is an online file storage service that lets you save pictures, videos and documents in the Cloud from your tablet and then access them on other devices. Content in your Dropbox can be shared with others, and is effectively backed up should anything happen to your tablet.

Wunderlist
This is a task manager that can organize your tasks into folders for easy viewing, create checklists, and set alerts for tasks. You can create new tasks from completed ones – a big time-saver given that many tasks are repetitive. Another useful feature lets you turn a list into a checklist.

Business Calendar 2
A handy calendar app with which to organize your life. Features include multi-day views, graphical or text view, multiple calendars, customizable widgets, recurring event options, and much more.

Alarm Clock Xtreme Free
To make sure you're always on time and don't forget to do things, the Alarm Clock Xtreme Free app is a worthy addition to your tablet. Features include a built-in timer, stopwatch, music alarm, crescendo alarm, and snooze button. The app is also highly customizable.

CHAPTER 10

Recreation

In Chapter 10, we see how you can use your tablet as an entertainment center. Not only can you take pictures and home videos with it, you can edit and organize them into albums to show to your buddies.

One of your tablet's best features though, is its ability to play video and music. Movies, TV shows, and music can be bought and downloaded from the Play Store and then played wherever you happen to be – a plane, a train, the bus – it doesn't matter.

Photography

Tablets are great devices for viewing your pictures. However, before you can do so, you need to get them on to the tablet in the first place. The main ways of doing this are:

● Taking the pictures with the tablet's camera

● Uploading the pictures from a computer

Taking Pictures With the Camera
Virtually all tablets provide at least one camera. Most provide two – a main rear-facing camera, and one at the front for video calls and so called 'selfies'. The former produces the best quality images.

On many tablets, the Camera app is on the Favorites tray; if not it will be on the Apps screen. Tap to open it and reveal the cameras settings. Note that these vary depending on the manufacturer of your tablet so may not be the same as shown below:

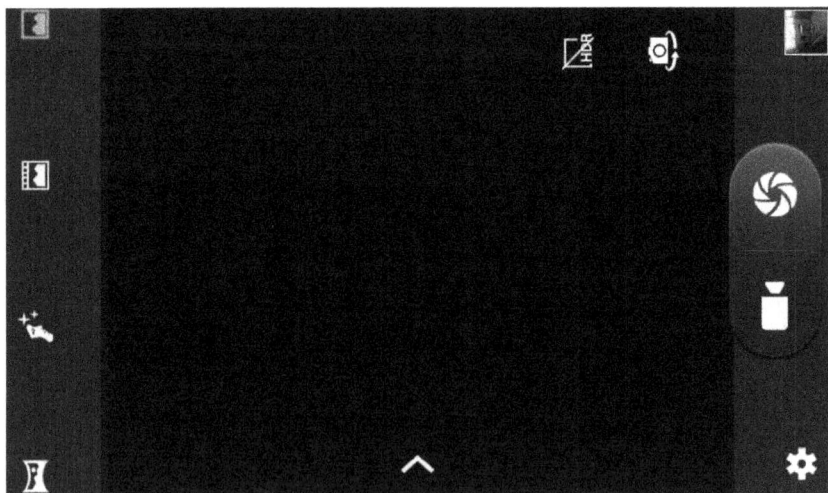

Working clockwise from bottom-left, we have:

● **Multi angle view mode** – this lets you photograph the subject from different angles and results in what is, effectively, a short video

cont'd

- **Panorama mode** – Panorama mode takes a number of pictures and stitches them together to create one wide image

- **Face beauty mode** – this feature attempts to 'beautify' the subject's face by removing facial flaws as far as possible in order to get a smoother and clearer face. Not surprisingly, the finished picture can look somewhat artificial

- **Live photo mode** – this is a feature that lets you share your experiences with friends and family by creating photos that launch short personal videos on a smartphone or tablet.

- **Normal mode** – choose this mode when you just want to take a normal unembellished, unenhanced picture

- **HDR** – HDR stands for High Dynamic Range image and the feature combines three pictures, each shot at a different exposure. The best parts of these images are then combined in one image that brings out details in both the shadows and the highlights – information that would normally be lost in a single exposure

- **Camera select** – this control lets you switch between the two cameras

- **View photos** – assuming you have taken some, tapping the image thumbnail at the top right-hand corner opens your picture folder. View them by swiping left and right

- **Picture mode & video mode** – moving down the right-hand side, there is the Shutter button that takes pictures and, below it, the video button that lets you shoot a video

- **Settings** – at the bottom left-hand corner is a gear wheel shaped Settings button. We look at these settings on the next page

- **Options** – situated at the bottom-center, tapping the Options up-arrow reveals four settings as shown below:

Working from left to right, the first lets you set the exposure manually, the second offers a choice of six filters with which to add a dramatic effect, the third lets you adjust the white balance, and the fourth lets you choose from various 'auto scene' modes, such as Night, Sunset and Portrait.

Camera Settings

Many users will be quite happy to use their tablet's cameras at the default settings. However, you may want to take a look at these settings to see if your use of the cameras can be improved. If so, tap the gear wheel Settings button to see what options are available:

The Settings window opens in the view shown on the right and provides three options. The first lets you specify the storage location for pictures and videos taken with the tablet's cameras.

The second, 'Image properties' opens a sub-window that gives you Low, Medium and High options for setting image sharpness, hue, saturation, brightness and contrast.

Store location	O
Image properties	Default
Anti-flicker	Auto
Restore defaults	

The third, Anti-flicker, lets you reduce, or eliminate, banding on videos.

Tapping the Camera button in the middle opens a window that provides a number of options and adjustments

These include enabling/disabling features such as Face detection, HDR and Auto scene detection.

You can also configure the Self timer for taking 'selfies' and set the picture size and the picture preview size.

Auto scene detection	O
Self timer	
Capture number	40 shots
Picture size	5M pixels

The button at the right lets you make some adjustments with regard to video. The first setting is EIS and it minimizes blurring and compensates for device shake.

You can turn the microphone On or Off and switch the audio mode between Normal and Meeting.

The Video quality setting lets you set the quality of the video to Low, Medium, High or Fine.

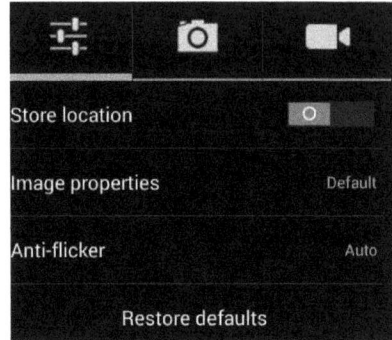

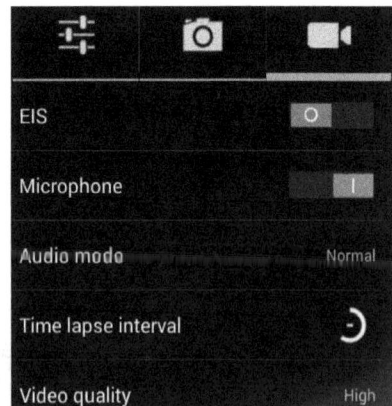

EIS	O
Microphone	I
Audio mode	Normal
Time lapse interval	
Video quality	High

Uploading Pictures to Your Tablet

While the cameras typically supplied with Android tablets take pictures of decent enough quality, those taken by a digital camera are definitely of a higher standard. However, where tablets do shine is their large screen, which is much better at displaying pictures than the small, low-resolution screen offered by the typical digital camera.

For this reason, many people use a digital camera to take their pictures and then upload them to a tablet for showing to friends and family. There are several ways this can be done:

Uploading from a Computer to the Tablet
The first is to upload the pictures from a computer to your tablet. In the procedure below, we are using a Windows 8 computer:

1. Connect your tablet to the computer with the supplied USB cable

2. On the computer, open the folder that contains the pictures to be uploaded, select them and then click Copy

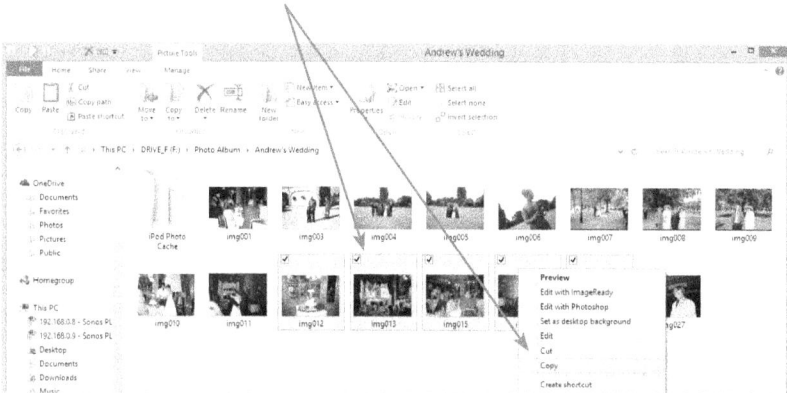

3. Go to 'This PC' or 'My Computer' and click your tablet. This will open the tablet's internal storage

4. Tap the Pictures folder to open it and then click Paste

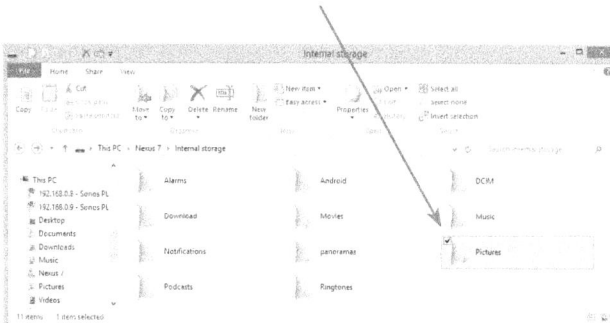

Uploading from a Card Reader to the Tablet

This is very similar to uploading from a computer. In this case, however, you need a card reader device such as the one shown below:

Take the memory card containing the pictures out of the camera and plug it into the card reader. Then connect the reader to your tablet. Android will recognize the device for what it is and allow you to browse through it for the required pictures.

Select the pictures and then copy them to a folder on the tablet. You can use any folder you like but we recommend you use the Pictures folder.

Copying From Email

This is a useful method for copying small quantities of pictures to your tablet:

1. Open the email that contains the picture

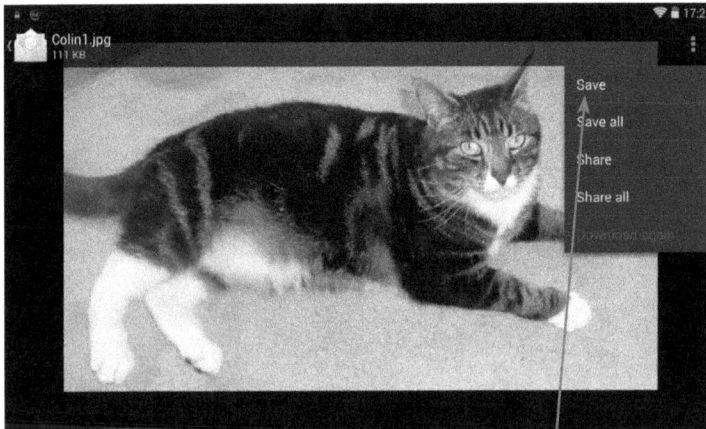

2. Tap the picture to open it, and from the Options menu at the top-right tap Save

3. The picture is saved to the Download folder

Photo Albums

Having got some pictures on your tablet, you will now want to take a look at them. To do so, tap the Gallery app on the Apps screen. The app keeps all the pictures and videos you shoot together in one place. This makes it easier to find them later when you want to view, edit, or share them with someone else.

To make specific pictures easy to locate, they are separated into albums; three of which are provided by default. These are: Camera, Pictures and Download. You can also create your own albums as we explain below.

When you first open the Gallery app, it opens in the Albums view:

Pictures taken with the tablet's camera will be in the Camera folder, pictures uploaded from a computer or card reader will be in the Pictures folder (assuming this is the folder you copied them to), and pictures copied from emails will be in the Download folder. Note that you will only see these albums if there are pictures in them.

Tapping the down-arrow to the right of Albums at the top-left of the screen provides two alternative views of your pictures – by Location and by Times.

Creating Albums

To create albums yourself, you need to connect your tablet to a computer as described on page 125. Open the tablet's internal storage, right-click on it and click 'New Folder'. Right-click on the new folder, click Rename, and enter the desired name. Remember though, you won't see your new album in the Gallery app until you place at least one picture in it.

Viewing Pictures

To view a picture, tap on the album that contains it. The album will open with the pictures displayed in a Grid view as we see below:

To view your pictures, just tap once on them. To zoom in by a set amount, tap twice on the opened picture – tap twice again to zoom back out. You can zoom in more precisely by placing two fingers on the picture and spreading them apart – pinch your fingers together to zoom back out.

To move from one picture to another, swipe left and right. To return to the album view, tap the arrow at the top-left of the screen.

You can also view your pictures in a different view called Filmstrip. To do this, tap at the top left-hand corner of the screen to open the menu shown on the right – select Filmstrip view.

cont'd

Tap once on an open picture to reveal options at the top right:

At the far top-right, you will see a ⚏ button – tap it to open the menu shown on the right. Options include:

Delete – tap this to remove the picture from your tablet. You will be asked to confirm the deletion.

Slideshow – this option lets you view all the pictures in the album as a slideshow.

Rotate left – rotates the picture to the left in 90 degree steps.

Rotate right – rotates the picture to the right in 90 degree steps

Crop – see page 131.

Set picture as – this option lets you set the picture either as wallpaper or as a contact's photo. Wallpaper options include the Lock screen and the Home screen.

Details – this opens a window that gives you the lowdown on the picture's specifications. These include dimensions, name, file size, camera details, and where the picture is stored.

Print – The final option, Print, we look at on page 132.

Also at the top-right is the ⚏ button, which opens the options shown on the right. These let you share and use your pictures in a variety of ways.

For example, tapping the Bluetooth option will let you send the picture to a nearby Bluetooth device; Email and Gmail will let you insert a picture into the body of an email; and Drive will let you save the picture online with Google Drive.

Note that the options available on this menu depend on the apps you have on the tablet. For example if you install the Evernote app, this will be available as well.

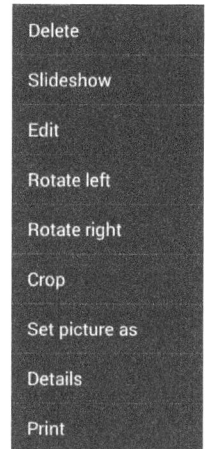

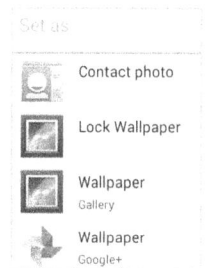

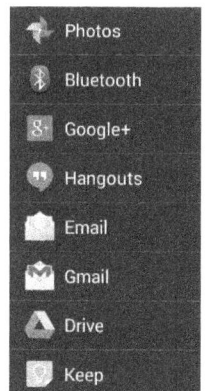

Editing Pictures

Not only can you take and store pictures on your tablet, you can also edit them. Tap the Gallery app and then open the picture to be edited. Tap the pencil icon at the bottom left-hand corner to open the Edit screen:

In the left-hand window, you see the image and how the editing affects it. On the right, you see the various editing tools. These are:

Color Filters
The Color filters button opens a filmstrip that offers a choice of nine color filters.

These can be used to apply a range of interesting lighting effects to the picture.

Frames
The Frames button also opens a filmstrip. Here, you will find a number of framing options for the picture.

Some are simple preset frames while others can be configured in terms of thickness, corner size, and color.

cont'd

Exposure

The Exposure  button lets you choose from a number of preset exposure settings.

These settings can all be adjusted by dragging the slider that opens at the bottom to the left and the right.

More Options

The More Options  button provides just that – more options. These comprise:

- Crop
- Straighten
- Rotate
- Mirror
- Draw

The Crop tool places selection handles on each side of the picture – drag the handles to resize the picture and crop out the unwanted section as shown on the right.

When you take pictures, sometimes it can be difficult to frame it so that it's level in relation to the horizon. The Straighten tool lets you straighten an image so that the horizon in the image is parallel to the bottom and top edges.

The Rotate tool lets you rotate the picture through 360 degrees in 90 steps.

The Mirror tool creates a reversed, mirrored image of the picture in a specified direction.

The final tool, Draw, provides you with a pen that can be used to make annotations on the picture. Adjustments include the type of pen, ink color and the size of the stroke.

Remember to save your edits by tapping the Save  button at the top-left.

131

Printing Pictures & Documents

It is possible to print pictures and documents from your tablet. The method we describe here lets you use absolutely any printer – it doesn't have to be Wi-Fi or Bluetooth. However, you will need a Google account, and also have the Google Chrome browser installed on your computer.

Setting up
The first stage is to register your printer with Google Cloud Print:

1.   Switch your printer on

2.   Launch Google Chrome on your computer and click the Options menu button at the top-right corner of the screen

3.   Click Settings and then click 'Show advanced settings' at the bottom

4.   In the Google Cloud Print section, tap Manage and then click 'Add printers'

6.   Login to your Google Account to enter Google Cloud Print

7.   A confirmation message appears on the next screen. This will register the printer that is connected to the computer. Click 'Add Printers' to confirm. Your printer is now registered with Google Cloud Print

Google Chrome will now act as a go-between for your printer and Google Cloud Print. When you print something from your tablet, you send data from it to Google Cloud Print, which forwards it to Google Chrome, which in turn tells your computer to print the document on the attached printer.

So, to print via Cloud Print, always make sure that your computer is connected to the Internet, that you are logged in to your Google account in Google Chrome, and that your printer is switched on.

Printing
Open the document, email, picture, or web page to be printed, and tap the Options menu at the top-right of the screen. Then tap Print to open the print options window.

Right at the top, make sure your printer is selected; if not, tap to open a drop-down list and select it from there.

The other options let you set the orientation of the document, media size, paper size, color and the number of copies. When everything is ready, tap the Print button at the bottom.

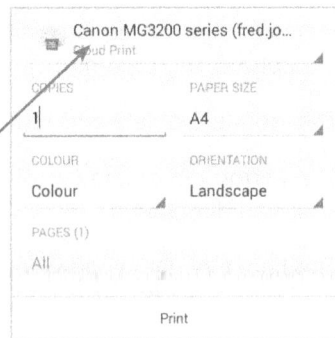
Canon MG3200 series (fred.jo...
Cloud Print

COPIES	PAPER SIZE
1	A4
COLOUR	ORIENTATION
Colour	Landscape
PAGES (1)	
All	

Print

Recording Home Videos

Although they are not the ideal devices with which to record video due to their somewhat awkward dimensions, a tablet will do when nothing better is to hand.

To record a video:

1. Open the Camera app

2. Select the required camera – either the higher quality front-facing camera or the lower quality rear-facing camera

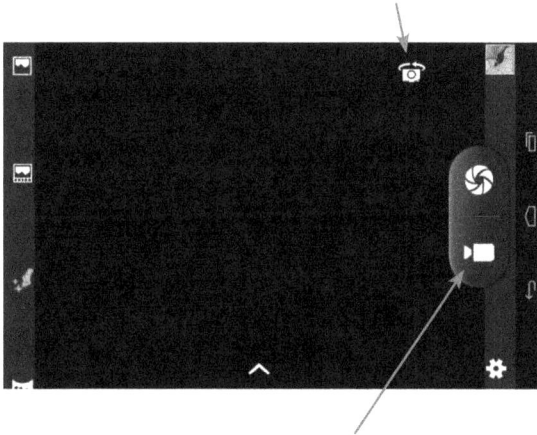

3. Tap the Record button to commence recording your video

4. At the bottom-left of the movie window, you'll see a timer showing the length of time you've been recording, plus a Pause button

5. To stop recording, tap the Record button again - the video is automatically saved

Locating Your Home Videos

All home videos recorded with an Android tablet are stored in both the Gallery app and the Videos app. So when you want to find these videos, this is where to go.

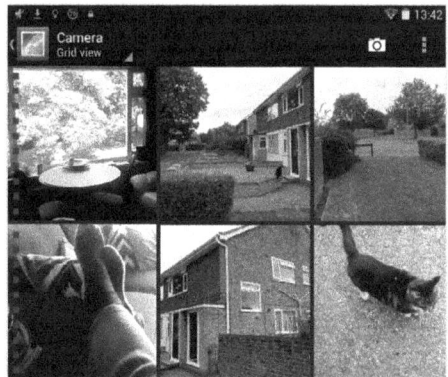

If you go to the Camera album in the Gallery app, you will see thumbnails of all pictures and videos taken with the cameras.

You can distinguish between them by the filmstrip placed on video thumbnails (with some tablets, there may be an arrow-in-a-circle icon).

Uploading Video From a Computer

On page 125 we explained the procedure for uploading pictures from a computer to your tablet. The procedure for uploading video is much the same. However, it is a fact that Android tablets are quite limited with regard to the video formats they will play. There are dozens of these formats but Android will only play videos encoded in the H.263, H.264, AVC, MPEG 4, and VP8 formats.

So before you upload a video to your tablet, you must first check that it is in one of the above formats. To do this, find the video file on your computer, right-click on it and click Properties.

The format will be listed next to 'Type of file' – .AVI in the example above. If the video is in an incorrect format, you have two options: The first is to download a video converter to your computer and use this to convert the video. Alternatively, you can download a video app to your tablet which will be able to decode the video as it plays.

Some video apps you can try for this purpose include: Mobo Player, VLC for Android, VPlayer, and MX Video Player.

When your video is suitably formatted, upload it as follows:

1. Connect your tablet to the computer with the supplied USB cable

2. On the computer, open the folder that contains the video to be uploaded, select it and then click Copy

3. Go to 'This PC' or 'My Computer' and click your tablet. Then click Internal Storage to access the tablet's internal storage

4. Tap the Movies folder to open it and then click Paste

5. You will see a message saying your device may not be able to play or view this file – disregard it by clicking Yes

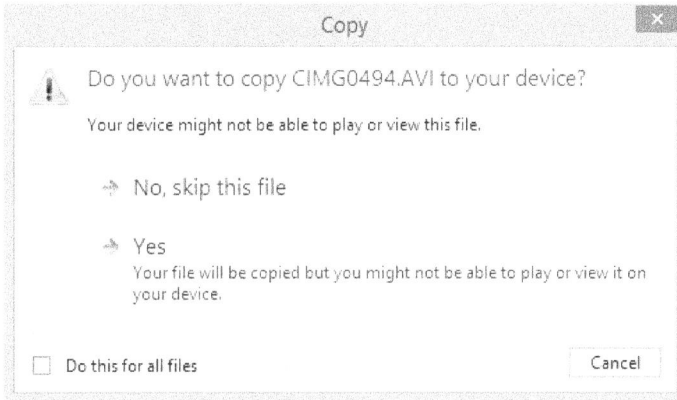

6. The video will now be uploaded to your tablet

Playing Videos

To play a video on your tablet that has been uploaded from a computer:

1. Open the Videos app

2. You will see a thumbnailed list of all your videos

3. To play a video, simply tap on it once – playback will commence

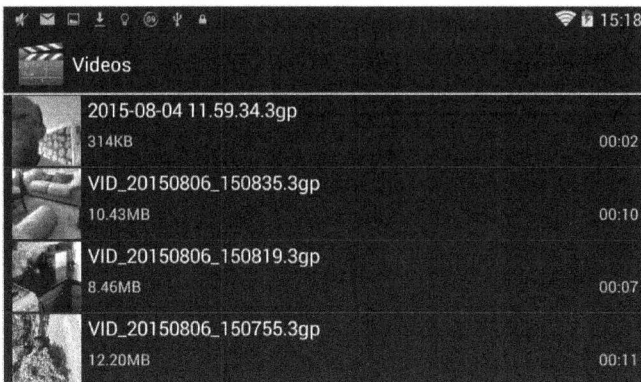

4. If you tap on the video while it is playing, a timeline will open below. You can use this to move about in the video and skip sections

Downloading Movies & TV Shows

While you can keep yourself amused with home videos, another feature of your tablet takes things to a different level. This is its ability to play feature-length movies and TV shows.

These are available from the Play Store and can be downloaded as follows:

1. On the Home screen, tap Play Store

2. At the top of the opening screen, you'll see a search box. If you know exactly which movie you want, use this to go straight to it. Otherwise, tap MOVIES & TV

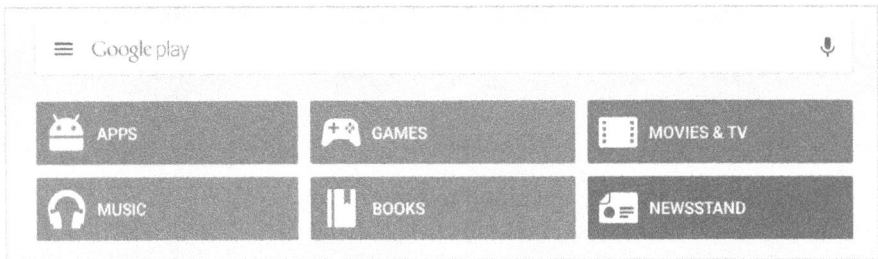

3. A new screen will open showing a number of categories at the top which you can use to just generally browse about, or to narrow your search. Scroll down to see movies and TV shows listed in various sections such as Top Selling, Most Popular, Recommended, etc

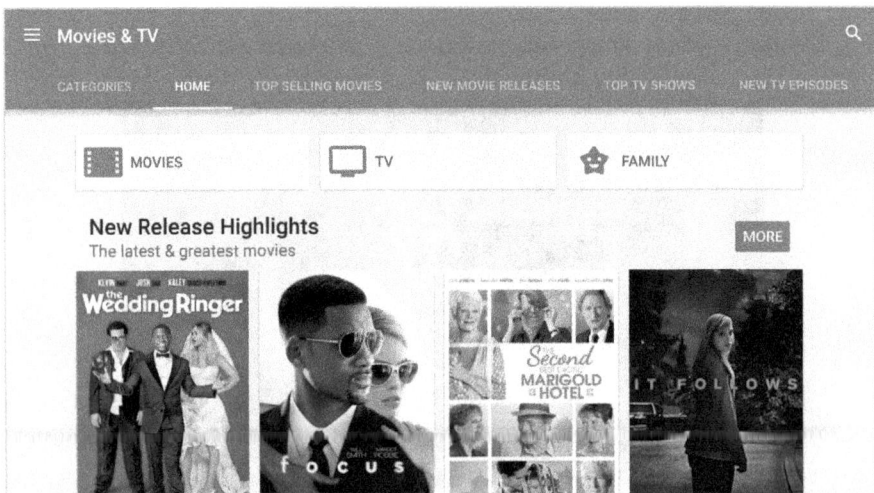

4. Having found something of interest, tap to open it in a new window

5. This gives you a summary of the plot, the cast, and info such as the producing studio, date of release, running time, etc. Other information includes Reviews, which lets you know how others have rated the movie, and Similar which gives you a list of similar movies. There may also be a brief preview at the top of the window, which you can play by tapping the arrow button

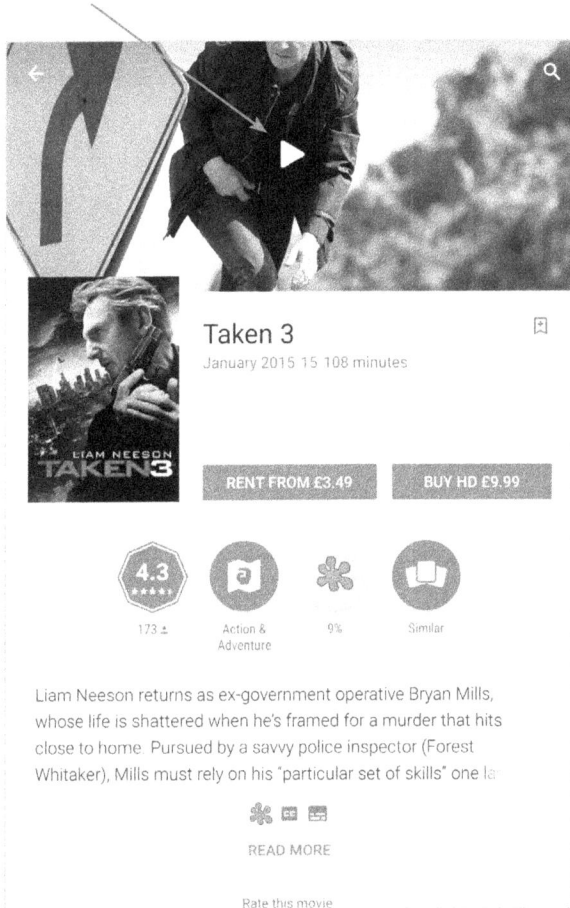

Taken 3
January 2015 15 108 minutes

RENT FROM £3.49   BUY HD £9.99

4.3

173 ±   Action &   9%   Similar
          Adventure

Liam Neeson returns as ex-government operative Bryan Mills, whose life is shattered when he's framed for a murder that hits close to home. Pursued by a savvy police inspector (Forest Whitaker), Mills must rely on his "particular set of skills" one la

READ MORE

Rate this movie

6. If you decide to rent or buy the movie, tap the appropriate button. If you haven't yet registered a credit card with Google, you'll have to do so now in order to continue.

    Payment methods
    stuartpeteryarnold@gmail.com

    Add credit or debit card

    Add PayPal

    Redeem

    When you have paid for the movie, tap the Download button. It will now download to your tablet where it will be available for offline viewing

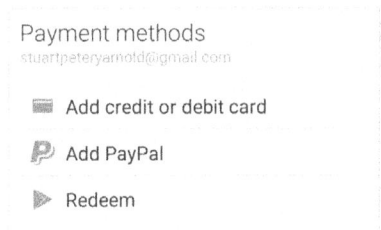

Watching Movies & TV Shows

Having purchased/rented a movie or TV show, you can then watch it on your tablet. You won't need an Internet connection to do it either – this is one of the great things about tablets – once it is on the device, you can watch the movie at any time and wherever you happen to be.

1. Open the Apps screen

2. Tap 'Play Movies & TV'

3. The app opens in the 'Watch Now' view, which shows your most recently downloaded movie at the top of the screen.

   Simply tap on it to commence playback – tap again to pause it

4. At the top-left of the screen is a three-bar icon – tap this to open the menu shown on the right

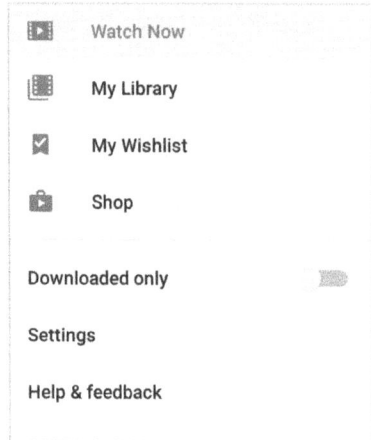

▶	Watch Now
▤	My Library
☑	My Wishlist
🛍	Shop
Downloaded only	
Settings	
Help & feedback	

5. To see all the movies and TV shows on your tablet, tap 'My Library'. You will see a thumbnail view of everything on the device

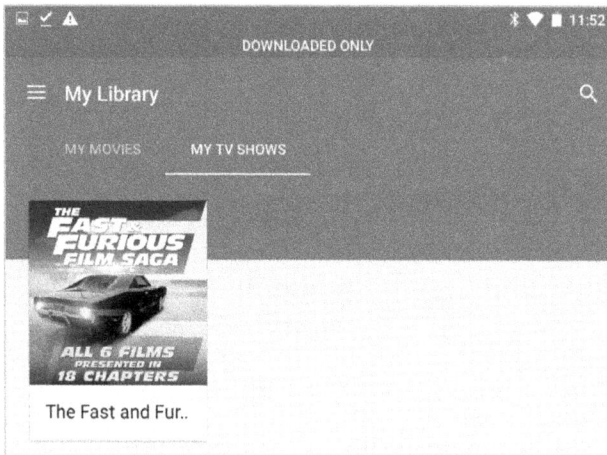

6. Tap on a movie to open a screen showing the movie's details. Tap on the thumbnail to play it. At the top-right is a button; tap it to reveal an option that allows you to delete the movie from your tablet

If you possess an HDMI cable, you can connect your tablet to a High Definition television and watch your downloaded movies and TV shows on the TV.

Getting Music on to Your Tablet

You can get music on to your tablet by uploading it from a computer, or downloading it from the Play Store.

Uploading From a Computer

The procedure for doing this is much the same as for pictures and video. However, unlike with video, you won't have to worry about the format issue – Android tablets will play the most commonly used audio formats.

To do it:

1. Connect your tablet to the computer with the supplied USB cable

2. On the computer, open the folder that contains the music to be uploaded, select it, and then click Copy

3. Go to 'This PC' or 'My Computer' and click your tablet. Then click Internal Storage to access the tablet's internal storage

4. Tap the Music folder to open it and then click Paste

Downloading From the Play Store

Open the Play Store and at the opening screen, tap the Music button. The Music section of the store will open at the Home screen. Scroll down to see various sections such as Top Tracks, Greatest Hits, Compilations, etc.

At the top of the screen are tabs for Genres, Top Albums, New Releases and Top Songs. These enable you to find the type of music you are looking for. You can also use the Search feature at the top of the screen to locate something specific.

When you have found a piece of music you want to download, tap on it to open its details screen. Here, you can read a description of the music and the artist, read reviews, see other music from the artist, and similar music from other artists.

You will also see a button showing the price of the music – tap this to purchase it. If it is an album, you can scroll down to see all the individual tracks. These can all be bought individually.

Next to the price, you may also see a button that says SUBSCRIBE.

Tapping this takes you to the Google Play website where you can sign up for a subscription service.

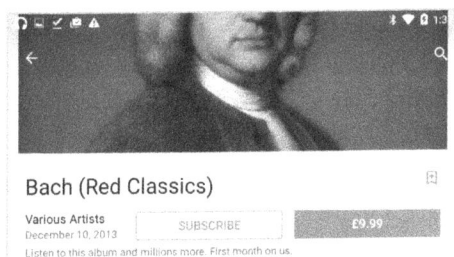

Bach (Red Classics)

Various Artists
December 10, 2013

SUBSCRIBE   £9.99

Listen to this album and millions more. First month on us.

Playing Music

Playing music on your tablet is, not surprisingly, done with the Play Music app. Open it and then:

1. The app opens in the 'Listen Now' view. This displays a list of music that has been recently played or added to the tablet

2. To play a track, tap on the thumbnail to open it and then tap the Play button

3. At the bottom of the screen, you'll see the controls

4. To see all your music, tap the three-bar button at the top-left of the screen and then tap 'My Library'

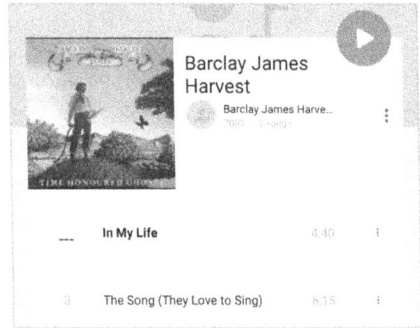

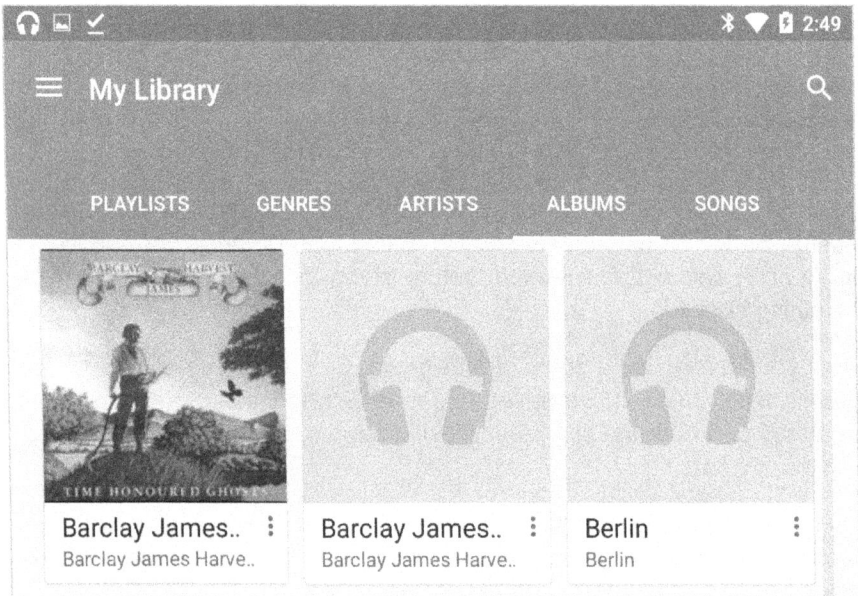

At the top of My Library, you'll see tabs for Playlists, Genres, Artists, Albums and Songs. Tap these to see your music collection organized in different ways. Whichever view you are in, the playback controls will be available at the bottom of the screen.

The Playlists tab shows a single Auto Playlist. This is created automatically and all the music on your tablet is added to this playlist. See page 143 for how to create your own playlists.

cont'd

Music Controls

The Play Music app provides you with a number of options when it comes to listening to your music:

Working from left to right, these controls take you to the beginning of a track, Play or Pause, and take you to the end of a track.

Tap to the left of the controls and more options will appear. At the top is an orange timeline – grab the button and drag it left and right to move about in the track.

Tapping this button will 'loop' the tracks that are currently queued. In other words, when the last one has finished playing, the first one will start again.

To shuffle, i.e. mix up, all the tracks in your music library, tap this button. They will then play back in a completely random order.

At the left of the music controls are thumbs-up and thumbs-down buttons. You can use these to rate the track on the Google Play website

At the top-right of the screen are two buttons. Tap this one to open a window showing a list of the currently queued tracks

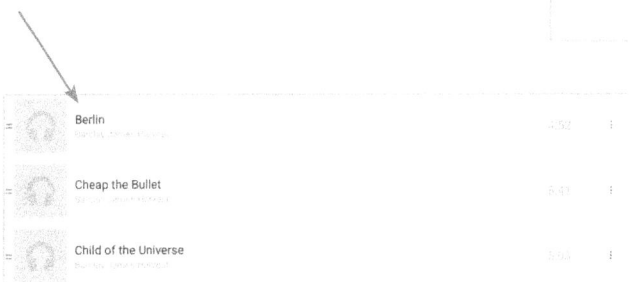

Berlin

Cheap the Bullet

Child of the Universe

Enhancing Your Music With the Equalizer

A useful feature of the Play Music app is the Equalizer. This provides you with a degree of control over how your music will sound. The Equalizer lets you adjust both the treble and bass output, and you can make the adjustments manually or with presets.

To use the Equalizer:

1. Open the Play Music app and start playing a track

2. Go to the 'Listen Now' view and tap the three-bar menu button at the top-left of the screen

3. In the menu, tap Settings and then tap Equalizer

4. At the top-right of the screen, tap the Equalizer's on/off switch to On

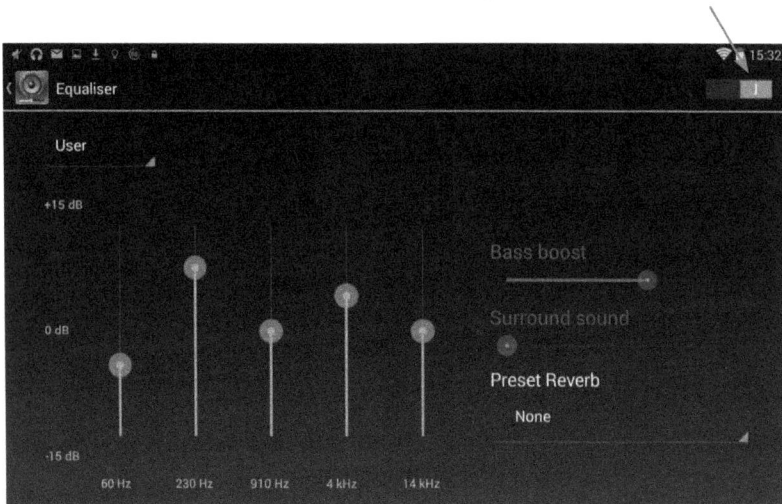

5. The Equalizer will now be activated. Drag the sliders up and down to adjust the bass and treble levels of the currently playing track

6. Tap the down-arrow at the right of User to open a list of presets. Any adjustments you make to these will be saved and applied the next time the preset is used

7. Also available is a Surround sound option and, depending on the track being played, a Bass boost option

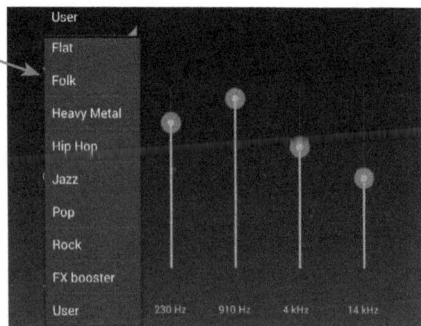

Organizing Your Music

The Play Music app provides two methods of organizing your music – the first is playlists and the second is queues.

Playlists

A playlist is a collection of tracks that is created to suit a mood or purpose. Once started, the music will keep playing through to the last track. DJs use them extensively.

To create a playlist on your tablet:

1. Open the Play Music app and go to the My Library view

2. Tap either the Playlists or Songs tabs

3. Pick a track to add to your playlist and tap the button at the right of it

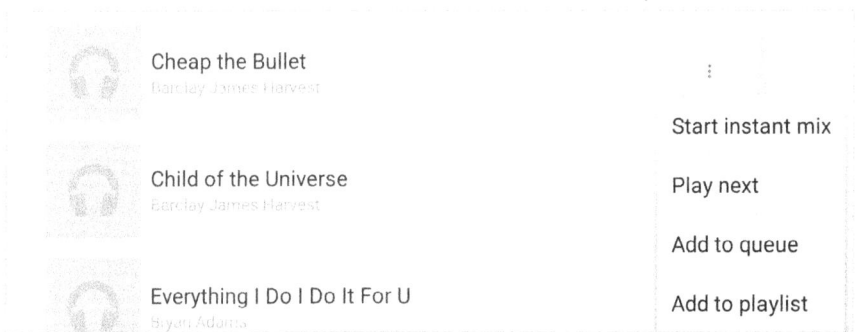

4. From the menu, tap 'Add to playlist'

5. In the window that opens, tap 'New playlist'. In the New playlist window, give the playlist a name. Then tap 'Create Playlist'

6. Repeat steps 3 and 4 to add more tracks to your playlist

7. When the playlist is complete, tap the Playlists tab at the top of the screen – the playlist will be listed together with the default Auto Playlist

8. Tap the playlist to open it and then tap the Play button to start playback

Queues

To queue a track, you add it to a playlist – essentially, what you're doing is modifying the playlist on-the-fly. Tracks that are queued are not added to a playlist permanently (unlike the playlist tracks) – when they have played, they are removed.

To queue a track, follow steps 1 to 4 above. In step 4, instead of tapping 'Add to playlist', tap 'Add to queue'.

Music Settings

Your Android tablet provides a number of settings, which enable you to manage the way the device is used to listen to music.

To access the settings:

1. Open the Play Music app

2. On the 'Listen Now' screen, tap the three-bar button at the top-left

3. Tap Settings – the Settings screen opens

We won't go into all of the settings but some we will mention include:

- **Google account** – tap this to sign-up for Google Play Music. This is a music streaming service that lets you listen to streamed music, not just on your tablet but also on other devices such as a computer, mobile devices and Android TV. 30 million tracks are available

  The full service requires a subscription to be paid at the end of the 30 day free trial

- **Start trial** – this also takes you to Google Play Music

- **My Devices** – this setting is related to Google Play Music as well. It lets you specify which of your devices to use when streaming music from the Google Play Music service

- **Block explicit songs in mixes** – when this setting is activated, any songs that contain explicit content will be blocked if you attempt to add them to a playlist

- **Cache during playback** – this option will cache (store) every track you stream from Google Play Music. This lets you listen to the music again later on when a connection is not available, i.e. you are offline. The downside is that it uses up storage space on your tablet. If this is a potential issue for you, deactivating the cache will delete any downloaded tracks and thus increase the available storage space

- **Automatically cache** – the Automatically cache option allows caching when your tablet is being charged and while it is connected to a Wi-Fi network. This helps to reduce the amount of data used

- **Clear cache** – tap this to clear the tablet's cache of any downloaded music tracks

- **Manage downloads** – tap this to open a screen from where you can monitor the progress of any items being downloaded to your tablet. You can also free up storage space from here

CHAPTER 11

Reading

Ebooks have arrived and are here to stay. While it is doubtful they will ever completely replace physical books, they do offer certain advantages and features that make them an interesting alternative.

For example, bookmarks mean you will never lose your page; people with poor eyesight can increase text size; you can make notes as you go along; you will never be short of something to read as long as you have a network connection, plus many more.

The Play Books App

When it comes to reading books on your tablet, the Play Books app is where you need to go. This app enables you to download and store literally hundreds of books across all genres on your tablet. They can then be read whether you're at home or out and about – it acts as your own personal library.

To get started:

1. Open the Apps screen and tap Play Books

2. The app opens in the Read Now view. If you haven't bought any books yet, the screen will be populated with a number of free and recommended books from the Play Store

3. When you have bought some, they are displayed as shown below:

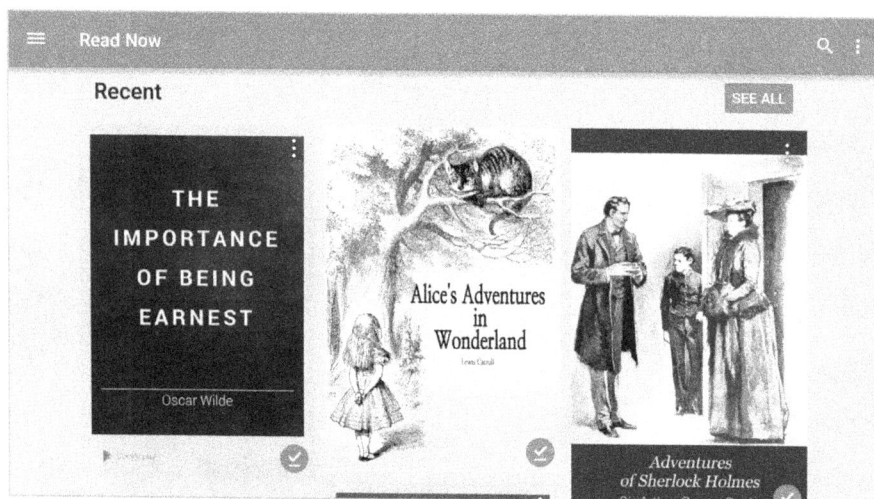

4. All books with a blue check icon have been downloaded to the tablet and thus can be read without having to be connected to a network. If they don't have the check, they are in the Cloud, i.e. the Play Store

At the top-left of the screen is a three-bar button – tap this to open a menu that offers several options. 'Shop' opens the Play Store from where you can download books; 'Downloaded Only' hides all books that are not actually on the tablet; and 'Settings' opens the app's Settings screen.

Also available from the menu are two app views – Read Now (the one shown in the image above) and My Library.

cont'd

Tap My Library to see a different view of your book collection:

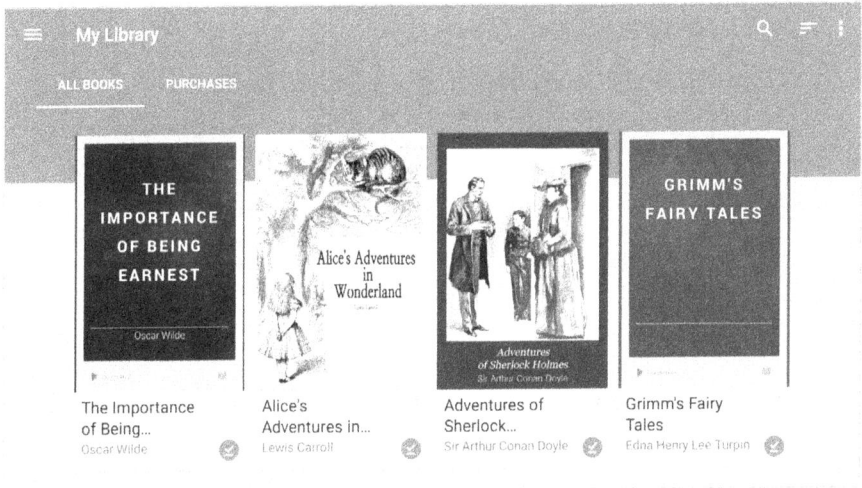

At the top-left are two tabs. All Books shows all the books on your tablet while the Purchases tab restricts the view to just those which have been paid for.

At the top-right are three buttons: the first opens a search box which takes its results from the Play Store's book section.

The second (middle) button opens a window that lets you sort your books by Recent, Title and Author.

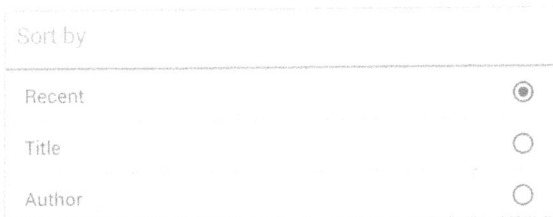

This can be very useful if you download a lot of books to the tablet.
The final button lets you refresh the screen – use this when you have downloaded a book but can't see it anywhere.

Finding Ebooks

As with all the other types of content you can download to your tablet, ebooks can be found at the Play Store.

1. On the Home screen, tap Play Store

2. The Play Store opens. At the top of the screen tap Books

3. You will see various headings such as Top Selling, New Releases in Fiction, Top Free, etc. Below, are sections such as Healthy Living, Book Club Reads and more

4. Tap the Categories heading to open a list of book categories. These will put you in the right ball park, so to speak

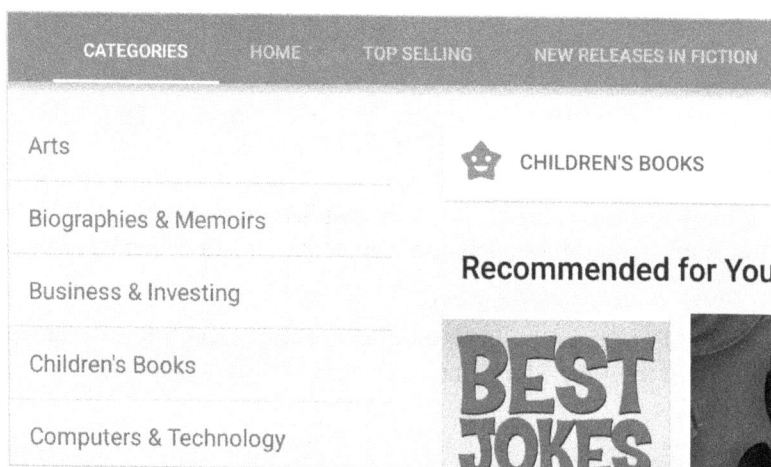

CATEGORIES	HOME	TOP SELLING	NEW RELEASES IN FICTION
Arts		⭐ CHILDREN'S BOOKS	
Biographies & Memoirs			
Business & Investing		**Recommended for You**	
Children's Books			
Computers & Technology		BEST JOKES	

If you are looking for something specific, it will probably be quicker to use the search box at the top-right of the screen.

Note that you are not restricted to the Play Store for your reading material. The Play Books app supports the EPUB format, which is used by many online book stores. For example, go to www.epubbooks.com and you will find an excellent selection of books that are in the public domain, i.e. are free.

You can also read Kindle books on your tablet. However, this cannot be done with the Play Books app – you have to download and install the Kindle app – see page 154. Once done, your entire Kindle library will be available on the tablet.

The same applies to books purchased from the Barnes & Noble bookstore. Just install the Barnes & Noble Nook app to read them on your tablet.

Previewing & Downloading Ebooks

Having found a book that may be of interest, you now need to take a closer look at it, particularly if payment is required.

1. Tap on the book to open its details page as shown below:

2. The first thing to look at is the book's precis, which gives a concise summary of its content. Then scroll down to read any reviews that have been left by other readers. Many books will also offer a free sample that you can read by tapping the FREE SAMPLE button

3. When you are sure that you want the book, tap the BUY button. In the window that opens, tap Continue

4. If you have already registered a credit card with Google, you will be asked to enter your password, after which the book will be downloaded. If you haven't registered a card, you will have do so now. Alternatively, you can pay with your Paypal account if you have one, or by redeeming a gift card or book token

5. Now open the Play Books app and you'll see the newly downloaded book at the top-left of the book shelf

Reading an Ebook

Unlike a physical book where what you see is what you get, with ebooks there are a number of options that let you control the book, and also tailor the display for a better reading experience.

Reading Options & Controls

Open the Play Books app and then select the book you want to read from your library. Then use the following options to read and control the book:

- **View a single page** – hold the tablet in Portrait mode

- **View two columns** – hold the tablet in Landscape mode

- **Turn to the next page** – either tap the right-hand side of the screen or flick to the left of the page with your finger

- **Turn to the previous page** – either tap the left-hand side of the screen or flick to the right of the page with your finger

- **Revealing the controls** – tap anywhere on the screen to reveal the controls – tap on the screen again to conceal them

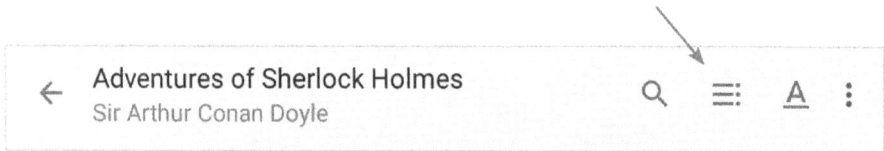

← Adventures of Sherlock Holmes
Sir Arthur Conan Doyle   Q   ☰   A   ⋮

- **View the table of contents** – tap to open the controls and then tap ☰ at the top-right of the screen. Tap on a chapter heading to go to it

CHAPTERS	BOOKMARKS	NOTES
Front Cover		i
Adventure I: A SCANDAL IN BOHEMIA		1
Adventure II: THE RED-HEADED LEAGUE		29
Adventure III: A CASE OF IDENTITY		60
Adventure IV: THE BOSCOMBE VALLEY MYSTERY		84
Adventure V: THE FIVE ORANGE PIPS		116
Adventure VI: THE MAN WITH THE TWISTED LIP		140

- **Move about in the book** – tap the screen to reveal the controls. Then, at the bottom of the screen, drag the dot on the slider left or right

- **Search the book for a specific word** – tap on the screen to reveal the controls and then tap the search button at the top-right of the screen. Enter the search term and then tap Search on the keyboard

The Play Books app provides you with a number of ways to view, alter and search the text in any book. You can also look up dictionary definitions and make notes as you go along.

Lets take a look at the available options:

Formatting Text
Text in all books uses a specific font – a set of printable or displayable characters in a specific style and size. With a physical book, the font cannot be changed but in an ebook, it can.

One of the most useful changes that can be made is the size of the font. For example, people with poor eyesight can increase it to a level that makes it much easier for them to read. To do this, and more:

1. Open the book and tap on the screen to reveal the controls

2. Tap the ⌂ button at the top-right

3. Tap the small T button to decrease the size of the font and the large T button to increase it. Below, you'll see two buttons that let you adjust the spacing between lines

4. Tapping the down-arrow at the right of Default lets you adjust the text justification to either Left or Full

5. To change the font itself, tap the down-arrow to the right of Original (the current font). This opens a list of alternative fonts that you can use

6. The Fonts menu offers some other options as well. Right at the top are three buttons that let you change the color of the background to White, Black or Sepia

7. Below the background buttons, you'll see a brightness control that lets you adjust the brightness of the screen. Tap the A button to the left of the slider to let the tablet set the brightness automatically

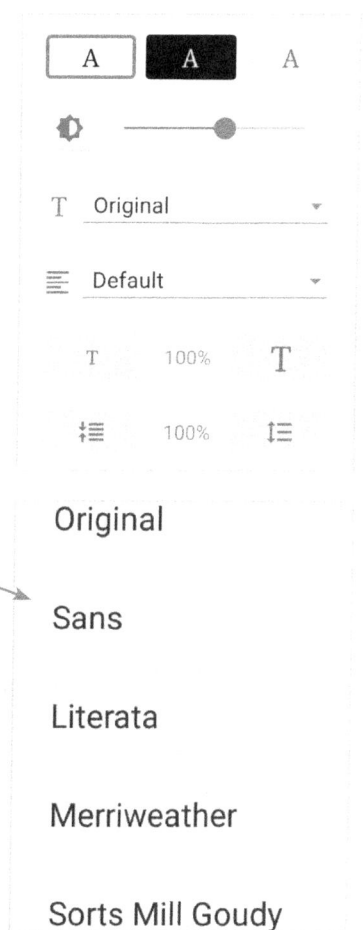

| A | **A** | A |

T   Original

☰   Default

T   100%   T

≡   100%   ≡

Original

Sans

Literata

Merriweather

Sorts Mill Goudy

Ebook Options

When reading an ebook, pressing and holding on a word brings up a toolbar that offers a number of options as shown below:

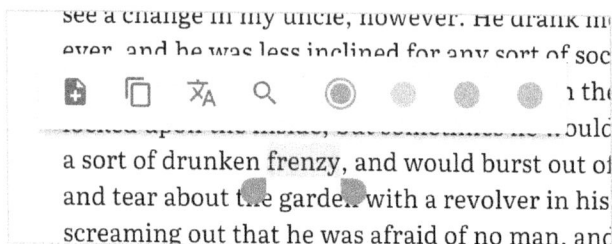

Working from left to right, these include:

Notes – tap the first button on the toolbar to open a new Note. The keyboard will open at the same time allowing you to enter text in the note.

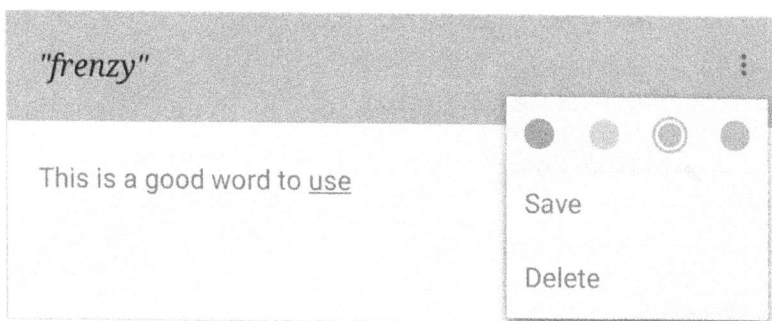

Having written the note, tap the button at the top-right to open an Options menu. Select a color for the note and then tap Save. You can also use this menu to delete notes.

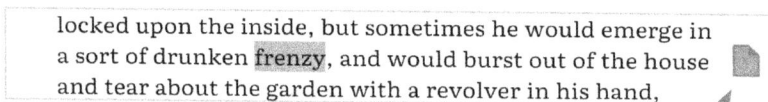

When you have saved the note, you will see an icon of matching color appear at the right of the page – tap it to open the note.

To view all your notes, tap on the screen to open the controls at the top and then tap the Table of Contents ≡ button. Then tap the Notes tab to open a list. To go to a note, just tap on it.

Copy – tapping the Copy button will copy the selected word, which you can then paste into a separate document or app. To do this, open the document or app, press and hold where you want to the word to go, and then tap Paste when it appears.

Of course, you may want to copy more than a single word. If so, grab the blue selection handles at either side of the selected word and drag them so that the required text is included.

Define & Translate – when this button is tapped, a window will open at the bottom of the screen offering a dictionary definition of the word:

> **frenzy**
> noun
> 1: a state or period of uncontrolled excitement or wild behaviour.

Tap the button again and you'll now see a Translate option. This lets you translate the word or phrase from any language to any language.

Search – tap Search to find other instances of the word in the book. At the top-right, you'll also see an option to search the web

Highlight – the final option gives you four colors with which to highlight the word or phrase

Bookmarks

When reading a physical book, we remember where we are by turning down the top-corner of the page or by inserting a bookmark. This functionality is built-in to ebooks and can be used in two ways:

● Tap the top-right corner of the page to be bookmarked. A blue bookmark icon will appear indicating the page is now bookmarked

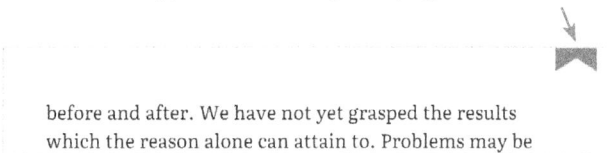

> before and after. We have not yet grasped the results
> which the reason alone can attain to. Problems may be

● Tap the screen to open the controls at the top. Tap the Options button at the top-right and from the menu tap 'Add bookmark'

To view your bookmarks, tap the Table of Contents button and then tap the Bookmarks tab.

Using Your Tablet as a Kindle

One of the biggest gripes from Kindle users is that the devices do not provide a color screen. They are also a touch on the small side. However, both of these issues can be resolved by using your tablet as a Kindle.

How? – all you have to do is install the Kindle app, which is available as a free download from the Play Store. Furthermore, if you already have a Kindle account, you can import your existing Kindle books to your tablet.

1. Open the Play Store and enter 'kindle' in the search box at the top-right of the screen

2. In the search results, tap on the Kindle icon to download and install it on your tablet

3. Open the Apps screen and tap the Kindle app to open it

4. In the 'Register this Kindle' screen, enter your email address and password

5. Under Library, tap All items

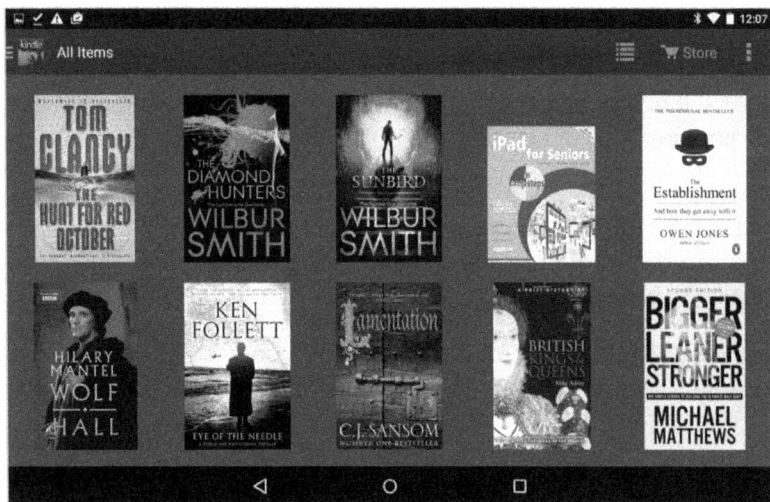

In the new window, you'll see all the books (if any) in your Kindle library – tap on one to download it to your tablet. Tapping 'All Items' at the top-left and then tapping 'On Device', will show you all the books actually on your tablet.

Tap the Store button at the top-right to access the Kindle Store from where you can find books, periodicals and magazines, and download them to your tablet.

CHAPTER 12

Google Now

Google Now is a free service provided by Google that is designed to supply useful information as and when it is required by the user. He or she doesn't have to ask for it – it just appears on their tablet. Many different types of information are available in the form of 'cards'.

In this chapter, we show you how to activate the Google Now service, set it up, the various information cards, and explain how to use them to receive real-time updates on a wide range of topics.

What is Google Now?

Google Now is a personal assistant developed by Google to compete with Apple's Siri. It can answer questions, make recommendations, and perform actions. Google Now proactively delivers to users information that it predicts they may want. This information is based on data that Google takes from a number of sources. These include:

- Your Internet browsing history

- Your location

- Your Google account

- Your calendars and email

When you activate Google Now, you authorize Google to access the information sources mentioned above, and also to activate Location Services on your tablet (this is off by default).

For Google Now to work, your tablet must be connected to the Internet via a Wi-Fi network.

Google Now Cards
Google Now delivers its information in the form of cards that are displayed on the tablet's screen. Each of these cards provides a specific type of information, e.g. sports results, weather, stocks & shares, etc.

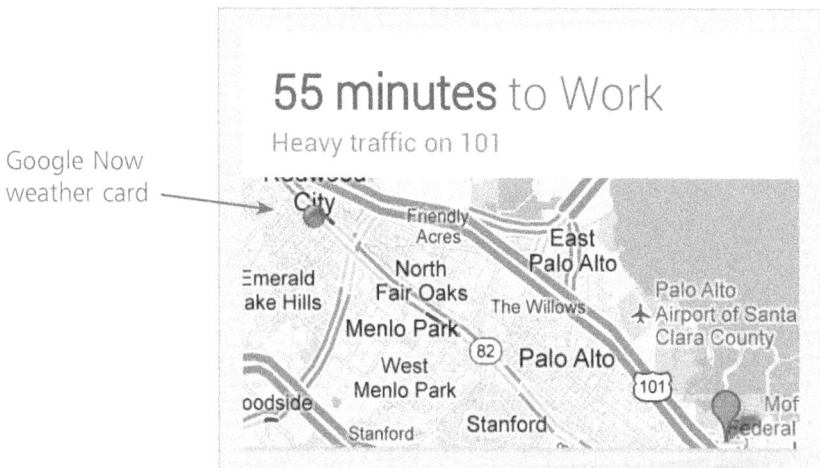

The user has no control over which cards appear or when – it's all determined by the data Google gleans from your account, web history and location. The latter is an important factor – for example, if you go abroad for a holiday, you'll get different cards than you do in your home country.

Activating Google Now

Google Now is a feature that not everyone is likely to use – for this reason it is deactivated by default. To activate it, do the following:

1. Swipe up from the bottom of the tablet to open the screen shown below:

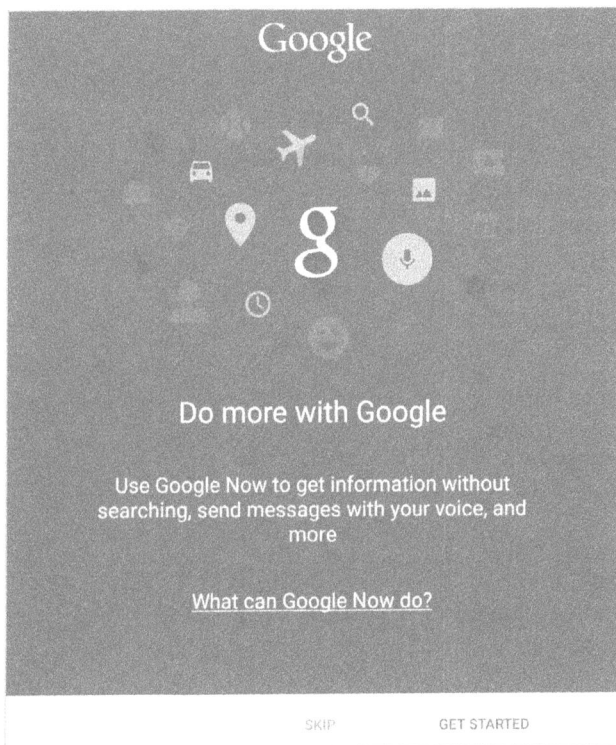

2. Tap GET STARTED to open the Set up Google Now? screen

3. In the Set up Google Now? screen, and the one that follows, you'll be advised which of your account settings will be turned on by Google Now; and the various types of information that it will require and where it will get them from. On both screens, you will need to give your approval by tapping YES, I'M IN at the bottom

4. Having done so, Google Now will now be activated and you will see its Home screen as shown on page 158

Note that Google Now runs silently in the background. You will only see it if you swipe up from the bottom of your tablet's screen or tap the Google app on the Apps screen. Normally, you won't be aware of it at all.

Exploring Google Now

When you've activated Google Now, its Home screen will open – this is where your information cards will be displayed. The ones you see initially depend on your location and other factors as already explained, but usually include a weather card and local news stories.

1. At the top of the Home screen is a Search box

2. Information card (the Weather card in this example)

3. If you see a More button, tap it to see what's available

4. Scroll down the screen to see all the available cards

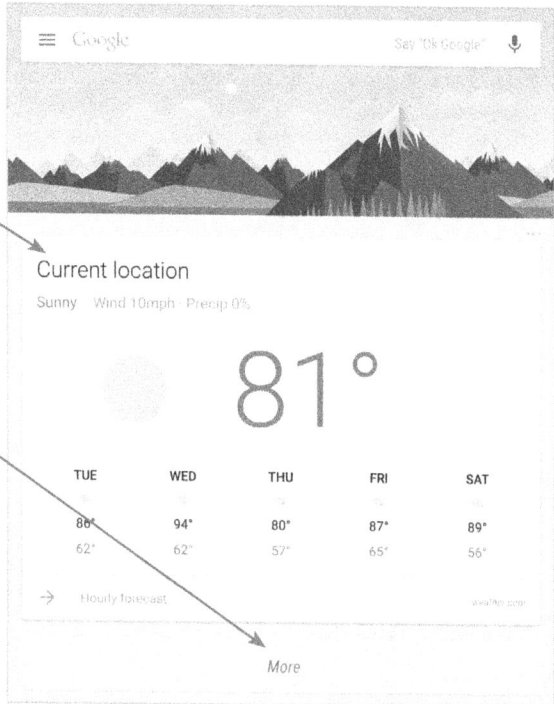

5. Tapping this button will open the card's settings. Note that all cards have their own settings

6. Tap the Forward and Backward arrows at the bottom to access the various settings screens for the card

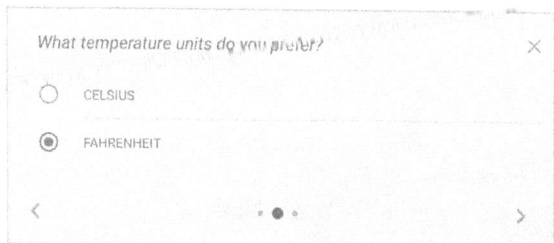

Customizing Google Now

As with most of the features on your tablet, Google Now can be turned on and off, and customized in various ways. This is done in its settings, which you can access by swiping to the right across Google Now's Home screen:

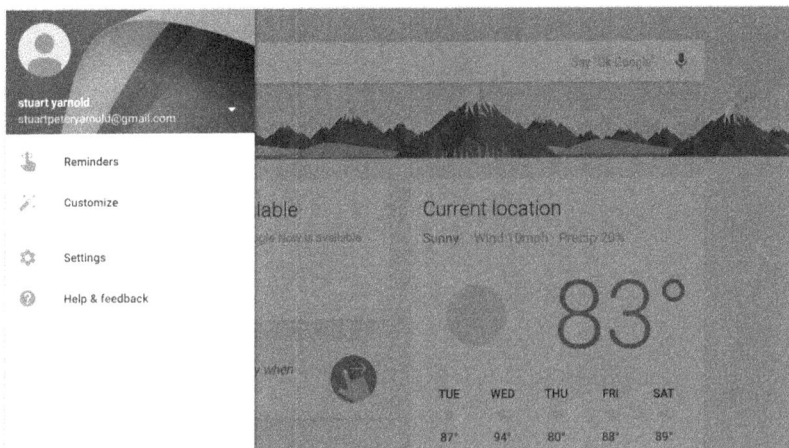

A menu will open at the left of the screen, where you'll see options for Customize and settings.

Customize
Tapping Customize gives you access to all of the different topics covered by Google Now — stock prices, places you've been to, sports teams, TV and radio programs and so on. The 'Everything else' category acts as a catch-all for information cards that don't fit anywhere else.

Once you get into a specific topic, you can tell Google Now what your interests are, the sports teams you follow, the movies you've watched, and so on. This lets you tweak the cards that are served up to a certain degree.

Settings
The Settings screen provides you with a number of options: Accounts & privacy let you specify which Google account is used by Google Now (assuming you have more than one). Tablet Search allows you to select which apps can return results for your on-device searches, such as Music and Chrome.

Probably the most useful setting is 'Now cards'. Here, you'll find sub-settings that let you turn off cards completely, manage your card history from a web interface, and turn off notifications for card updates (these appear on the Notifications bar).

Editing Google Now

Much of the information served up on Google Now cards is taken from the your Internet usage, or web history. Quite apart from the searches done via the Google search engine, info is also taken from any Google app that uses the Internet, such as email, Google Maps and Google Earth.

This web history can be accessed by going to **google.com/history** and signing in to your Google account.

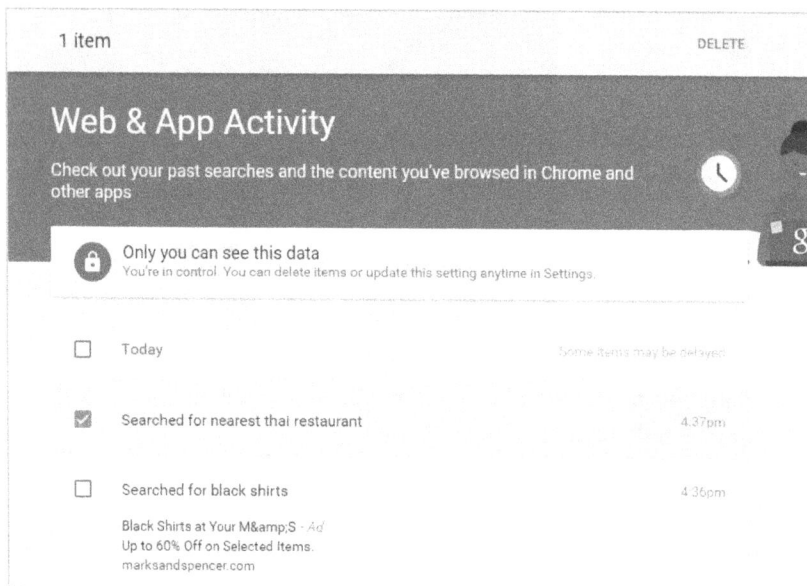

You'll see that your web history is saved on a day-by-day basis with each Internet activity being recorded individually. Alongside each activity is a checkbox that allows it to be selected. There is also a checkbox for each day that allows all the activities for that day to be selected.

All these activities are used by Google Now to fine-tune the information it presents to you. For example, a browsing session that includes Thailand and restaurants is quite likely to bring up a card showing local Thai restaurants – information that you probably don't want.

If this is the case, all you have to do is delete the activities that triggered the card. Just select them in your web history by checking their boxes and then click DELETE at the top-right of the screen.

The menu bar at the top-left provides a lot of useful options. For example, tap Location History and you'll see a map that shows you exactly where you and your tablet were on any specified day.

Google Now Cards

Google Now cards come in two types: the ones linked to Gmail accounts and the standard ones described in this chapter. We'll take a closer look now at some of the more useful examples of the latter:

Weather Card

By default, the Weather card gives you a five-day forecast for your home location. However, by going into the card's settings, you can change this to your work location or your current location.

The settings also let you specify whether or not you want weather updates, continue to get updates, and configure the card to show temperatures in Centigrade or Fahrenheit.

Current location

Sunny

81°

TUE	WED	THU	FRI	SAT
86°	94°	80°	87°	89°
62°	62°	57°	65°	56°

Tap 'Hourly forecast' right at the bottom to access a more detailed forecast.

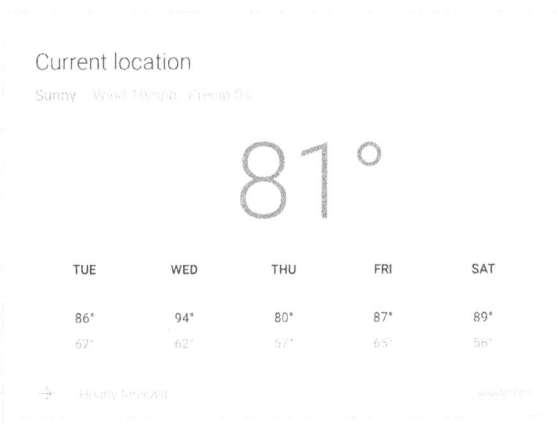

Traffic Card

A very useful transport-related card is Traffic. This shows you the prevailing traffic conditions for a specified route and how long the journey is likely to take.

At the bottom of the card, you'll see a Navigate button – tap this to get a list of directions. This will be taken from the GPS function in Google Maps.

51 minutes to LAX, 1 World Way, Los Angele...

Heavy traffic on I-110 S

The settings for the Traffic card allow you to specify your mode of travel: driving, walking, cycling or public transport. The information provided on the card is amended accordingly.

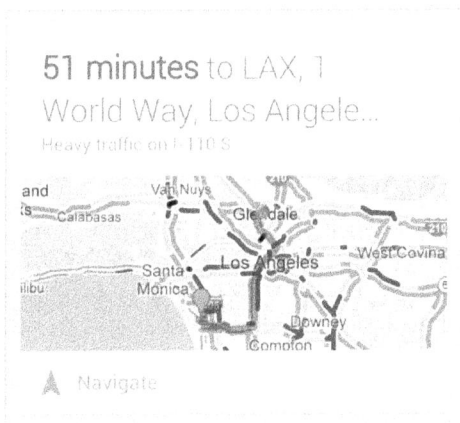

Navigate

Another transport-related card is Public Transport. This will appear whenever you are near to a bus or railway station and show details of schedules that are relevant to you and your current location.

Sports Card

A very popular card is Sports. You can use this to keep abreast of your favorite sports teams – news, schedules and results.

| Wake Forest | 28 |
| Duke | 27 |

1st, 08:15

	1	2	Total
Wake Forest	28	–	28
Duke	27	–	27

To specify which teams to feature on the card, go into the card's settings and tap 'Add a team'.

A window opens in which you can type the name of the team you want to add. Repeat this for all the teams in which you have an interest.

Stocks

Another very useful and popular card is Stocks. This provides up-to-date stock market news, trends and figures. To specify which stocks you want to monitor, go to the card's settings and just type in the relevant stocks.

TV & Video

When you search for a movie, TV show, music artist, or video game on Google, it'll remember and give you information about it in Google Now. You can configure Google Now to remind you about upcoming episodes, so you know when your favorite shows start. In the card's settings, you can specify your cable provider and on-demand services, such as Netflix and Hulu, and it'll adjust the card for those services.

If you have an network-connected TV, Google Now will detect the TV and you can tell it to 'listen' to what you're watching. It'll then provide you with more information about that show.

Flights

The Flights card keeps you updated with regard to arrivals and departures from the airport closest to your current location. It also tells you the traveling time to the airport.

The Google Now service is expanding rapidly and, at the time of writing, it had just teamed up with the manufacturers of over 100 apps. As a result, it is now offering cards with information from the likes of Runkeeper, OpenTable, ABC News, Feedly, Airbnb, Instacart, Lyft, Mint, Kayak, Ford and Gett.

If you have any of these apps installed on your tablet, the cards will appear automatically when they have information relevant to your current situation.

CHAPTER 13

Security

If you are like most other users, it won't be long before your tablet is jam-packed with information and data that is either highly personal and thus confidential, or simply too important to lose – indeed, maybe both.

To protect your data, the device provides a number of security features. These include password protection, backing up, and protection controls. In this chapter, we explain how to configure and use these features in order to keep your data safe and secure.

Security Issues

With more and more people using their smartphones and tablets to surf the web, update social networking sites, and shop & bank online, cybercriminals are increasingly targeting owners of these mobile devices.

Viruses

Unfortunately, these cyber attacks are aimed predominantly at Android devices. In 2013, over 85% of all mobile malware was designed to target the Android platform. The reasons for this are:

- Android is the most widespread operating system for mobile devices with some 70% of the market

- The open source nature of Android, the ease with which apps can be created, and the wide variety of (unofficial) app markets

- Android suffers from the issue of fragmentation – there are multiple versions of Android on the market

The solution to the issue of malware is to install an anti-virus app on your tablet. We look at how to do this on pages 165-166.

Loss

Another area of concern with regard to security is the simple issue of loss. Tablets are small devices that are easy to misplace or steal. The main concern for many in this situation is that their data will be accessible to whoever finds, or stole, the device.

Fortunately, there are solutions to this as well. First, your tablet has a feature that allows you to encrypt its contents, so even if it falls into the wrong hands, it won't be accessible. There are a number of apps that will let you lock the device remotely, and even delete all the data on it. We look at this on pages 170-171.

Content Restriction

There are many reasons why you may want to place restrictions on who can view your tablet's content, or part of. You may access websites that you would rather other people don't know about, or there may be children using the tablet.

The latter will be a particularly important issue for parents who will be keen to prevent their offspring from accessing unsuitable websites. Once again, the solution is to install a content restriction app, many of which are available in the Play Store. These allow you to specify precisely which apps (and thus content) can be accessed by other users of the tablet. Or, you can try the procedure we describe on page 169.

Viruses & Dealing With Them

As we noted on the previous page, Android devices are particularly vulnerable to viruses due to the nature of the operating system. For the uninitiated, a virus is a piece of malicious software that attacks electronic devices by compromising the operating system, thus enabling it to steal confidential information from the device.

There are three main types of virus known to attack mobile devices. These are:

Worms – the main objective of this type of virus is to continually reproduce itself and spread to other devices. They can be transmitted via text messages and, typically, do not require user interaction for execution

Trojans – unlike worms, a Trojan horse always requires user interaction to be activated. This kind of virus is usually inserted into seemingly innocuous apps that are downloaded to the device and then executed unwittingly by the user. Once activated, the Trojan can cause serious damage by infecting and deactivating other applications, or even the device itself

Spyware – this type of virus poses a threat to a user's data by collecting, using, and spreading their personal information without their consent or knowledge. There are various types of spyware, such as system monitors, adware, and tracking cookies

So, how do you protect your tablet against these threats? Well the obvious step is to install an anti-virus app as we'll explain shortly. However, the steps below will also provide a measure of protection:

- Use your tablet's data encryption feature. Doing so means that in the event of the device being compromised, criminals will not be able to access the personal information that's stored on it

- Be aware of permission and access requests from apps running on your tablet. It's particularly important to do this with Android smartphones

- Switch off Bluetooth. Bluetooth is a type of wireless network and it is effectively a doorway to your tablet. If you're not using your Bluetooth connection, switching it off means there is one less way for your tablet to be attacked. If it also has a 3G or 4G connection, the same applies

- Be very careful when handling email attachments. If you do not know the person who sent it, the best course of action is to simply delete the email. Opening attachments is a common way to let viruses into your device

Anti-virus Apps

Anti-virus Apps

To protect your tablet against malicious attack from viruses, you need to install an anti-virus app. These apps work unseen in the background, constantly monitoring what's happening on the tablet for any signs of suspicious activity.

But which one? A quick look in the Play Store will reveal a huge number of these apps and you will find it quite a task to decide which one to use. To save you the bother, we've done it for you. Our recommended list of anti-virus apps is:

- Avast Mobile Security & Anti-Virus

- Ikarus Mobile Security

- Kaspersky Internet Security

- Norton Mobile Security

These apps provide a similar level of anti-virus protection – there's little to choose between them in this respect. Also, they are all free but in order to access all their features, you will need to pay for the premium versions.

Where they do differ is the quantity of security features on offer. Avast Mobile Security & Anti-Virus, for example, literally bristles with tools that not only protect against viruses, but also let you remotely control your device in case of loss or theft, lock specific apps to prevent other people using them, erect Firewalls and much more.

In operation, they all work in much the same way. Once installed, they all immediately carry out a full scan of the tablet to identify any threats. Any that are found are either removed from the device or placed in 'quarantine' where they cannot do any harm.

From this point on, they work invisibly in the background and normally you will never even be aware of them. About the only thing you need to do is ensure the anti-virus app is updated periodically to make it aware of the latest security threats.

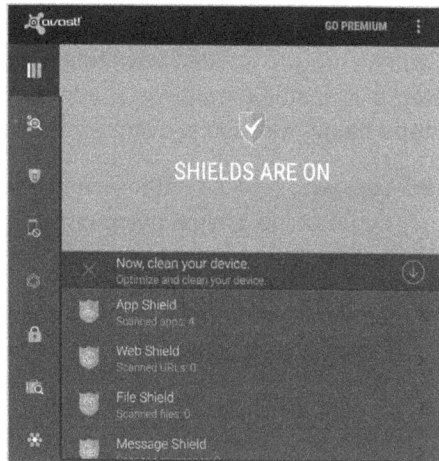

Locking Your Tablet

By default, Android tablets are supplied with little or no protection. If you don't take steps yourself to protect your device and the data on it, you run a real risk of having it compromised in any of a number of ways.

One such is the simple act of someone just picking up your tablet and nosing through it. Having installed an anti-virus app, this is the next thing to sort out and the way to do it is to lock the tablet with a password or code.

There are any number of apps in the Play Store that will do this for you but users of Android devices have this feature built-in to their device.

To use it:

1. Open the Settings app

2. In the Personal section, tap Security

3. At the top of the screen, tap 'Screen Lock'

You will see a number of options: None, Slide, Face Unlock, Voice Unlock, Pattern, Pin and Password. The first two, None and Slide, do not offer any protection – the others all do.

Tap Pattern and you will see a grid layout containing nine dots as shown on the right. Place a finger on one of the dots and then without taking it off the screen, trace a line that interconnects at least four of the dots.

Having done so, tap Continue and then, in the new screen, trace the pattern again. Then tap Confirm at the bottom of the screen.

If the Pattern option doesn't appeal to you, you can try Password. This opens a window in which you can type a password. Note that the password has to contain at least four characters. However, to provide a decent level of security, we suggest a minimum of eight characters including at least one number and punctuation mark.

The Pin option is very similar to Password. Instead of a keyboard with which to enter letters though, you will see a number pad. Tap a minimum of four numbers to create a pin number.

With any of these three options set, your tablet is locked. To enter the device, it will be necessary to specify the pattern, pin number or password before you can access the Home screen. Should you ever wish to remove the tablet's lock protection, repeat steps 1 to 3, and tap None. Your tablet will then be unprotected.

Data Encryption

If protecting the data on your tablet is very important to you, your best option is to encrypt it. Data encryption is the act of changing electronic information into an unreadable state by using algorithms and ciphers. Once encrypted, it must then be decrypted to make it intelligible – this requires a pin number to be entered first.

For users who want to encrypt their data, Android provides an encryption feature. To use it:

1. Charge your tablet fully – the encryption process will not start until it is

2. If you haven't already done so, create a lock screen PIN number or password as described on page 167

3. In the Settings app, tap Security in the Personal section.

4. Tap Encrypt tablet

5. You will see the following advisory message

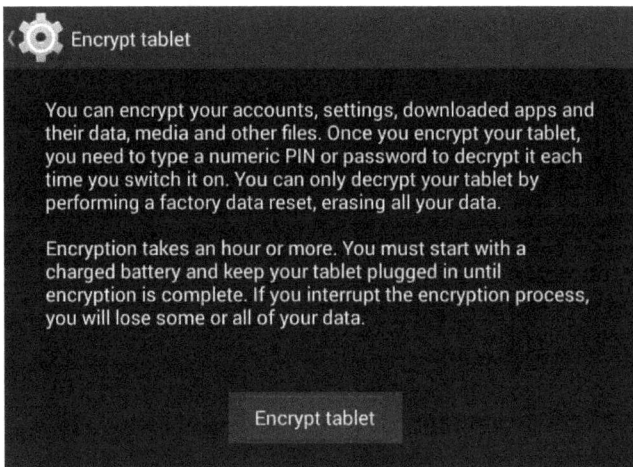

6. Tap the Encrypt tablet button to begin the encryption procedure

Before you encrypt your tablet, be aware that there are drawbacks:

● **Performance** – Encryption always adds some overhead, so your tablet will run a bit more slowly than it did before

● **It's permanent** – Encryption is one-way! After encrypting your tablet, it can only be unencrypted by restoring the tablet to its factory default settings. This will also erase all the data stored on it, so you'll then have to set it up from scratch

Content Restriction

If other people are going to be using your tablet and there are parts of the device that you don't want them to have access to, you need to set up content restriction.

However, Android does not provide an app with which to do this, so you will have to download one from the Play Store. Some typical examples are:

- Android Parental Control

- AppLock

- Screen Time

- Norton Family Parental Control

One that we recommend is AppLock. The first time you run the app, you are asked to specify a password, which will need to be entered each time the app is opened.

AppLock is very straightforward – listed on the main screen are all the apps on the tablet. Tapping on one immediately locks it – the password will be needed to unlock it.

The app also provides two vaults – one for pictures and one for videos. Just open one of the vaults, tap the + button at the bottom and you are taken to the Gallery app from where you can move the photos or videos to the vault.

Another very useful feature is Profiles. This lets you create Guest profiles and assign them to people who use the tablet. Within each profile, you can specify exactly which apps and functions can be used by the guest.

Finding a Lost Tablet

If you've simply misplaced the tablet, your only concern will be finding it. However, if it has been lost or stolen, you may also have to consider the implications of someone accessing your personal data, and what to do about it.

In both scenarios, the solution is provided by an app called Android Device Manager. This can be accessed at:

www.google.com/android/devicemanager

Before it will work though, you need to configure your tablet to use it as we describe below:

First, you need to make sure that your tablet's Location Service is switched on. To do this:

1. On the Apps screen, tap Settings

2. In the Personal section, tap Location

3. At the top of the screen, make sure the switch is in the On position

Next, you need to configure Android Device Manager:

1. Open the Apps screen and tap Google Settings

2. Tap Security

3. Under 'Android Device Manager,' move the switch next to 'Remotely locate this device' to the On position

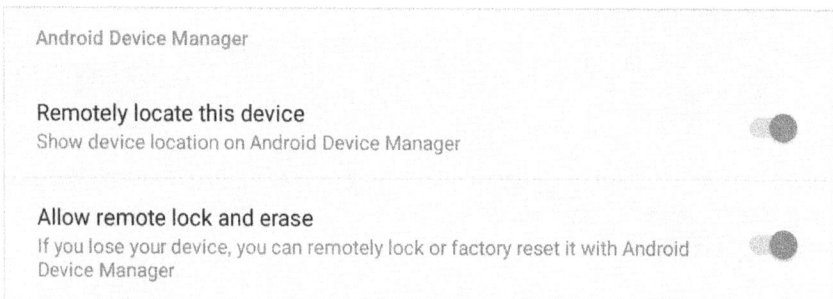

Android Device Manager

Remotely locate this device
Show device location on Android Device Manager

Allow remote lock and erase
If you lose your device, you can remotely lock or factory reset it with Android Device Manager

4. Move the switch next to 'Allow remote lock and factory reset' to the On position

Android Device Manager is now set up on your tablet. To test it, you will now need to open a web browser on a different computer or tablet and go to www.google.com/android/devicemanager

cont'd

You will be asked to log in to your Google account. Having done so, you will see a map as shown below:

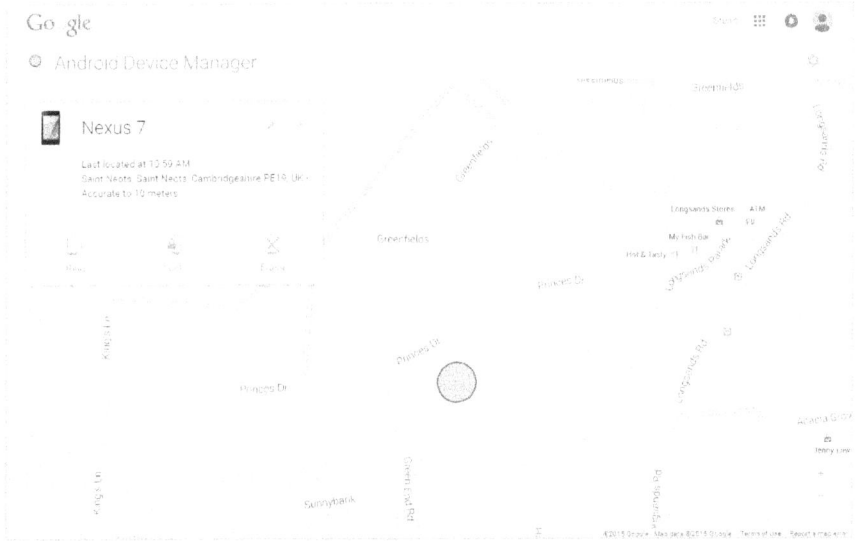

The blue circle pinpoints the location of your tablet on the map, and the information box at the top-left tells you the approximate address. Below this, you'll see three options: Ring, Lock, and Erase.

Click Ring and your tablet will ring for five minutes at full volume or until the power button is pressed – use this option if you have simply misplaced it.

Remotely Locking & Erasing a Tablet

The second option, Lock, you would use if the tablet has been lost or stolen. Click it to open a screen that lets you enter a password that will replace the existing password. Then click Lock to lock the tablet.

The last option, Erase, will erase everything on the tablet. When done, it will be just as it was when you first used it. All your pictures, apps, music, etc, will be deleted.

Users who have access to a separate Android device can use that device to find, lock and erase a missing tablet in exactly the same way. To do this, you will need to go to the Play Store on the second device and download the Device Manager app.

When it has been installed, tap OPEN. In the opening screen, you will be asked to sign in to your Google account. Do so and you will see the same map as above, along with the Ring, Lock and Erase options.

Backing Up & Restoring a Tablet

If you have anything on your tablet that you really would not like to lose, you need to create a backup of everything on the device. In the event of loss or theft, the important data can be restored from that backup.

Backing Up

By default, your tablet automatically creates backups at periodic intervals and one of these may be sufficient. However, you can create a backup yourself at a time of your own choosing as we describe below:

1. Open the Apps screen and tap Settings

2. In the Personal section, tap 'Backup & reset'

3. Tap Backup account

That's all you need do – a backup of your data, passwords and settings will now be created and stored on Google's online Backup Service.

Restoring

To restore your tablet's data and settings from a backup, you need to open the Backup & reset screen as above. Then:

1. Tap 'Factory data reset' – you will see a warning message advising that everything on the tablet will be erased – tap RESET TABLET at the bottom of the screen and then tap ERASE EVERYTHING

2. The tablet will now be wiped clean of all the data it contains and then reset to an 'as new' condition – the process will take a few minutes

3. When the reset is complete, you'll have to set up your Wi-Fi, sign in to your Google account, and agree to the Google terms of service

4. When you have signed in to your Google account, the data that you previously backed up for that Google account is restored to the tablet

With regard to app settings (not tablet settings), you can choose to restore these when you reinstall an app on your device. To do this, tap the 'Automatic restore' option in the Backup & reset screen.

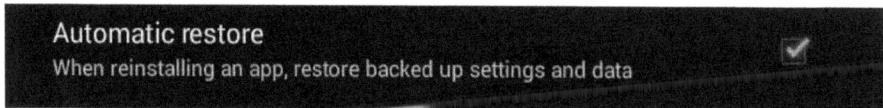

Automatic restore
When reinstalling an app, restore backed up settings and data

Note that because your backups are stored in the Cloud, they can be accessed on another Android device. This means that you can restore or set up that device from one of the backups.

CHAPTER 14

Third-Party Apps

The apps supplied with your tablet cover all the main applications that the device can be used for, e.g. email, browsing the Internet, listening to music, reading, etc. However, there are alternatives to all of them, many of which provide more, and better, features and options.

Then, of course, there are the applications that the default apps don't cover. Things like holidays, travel, property, finance and so on. In this chapter, we take a look at some third-party apps that may be useful to you.

Alternatives to Default Apps

Here, we are going to look at alternatives to two of your tablet's most used default apps – the Email app and the Internet app, Chrome. We'll begin with Email.

CloudMagic – with a light and clean design, CloudMagic is the email app of choice for productivity. It offers a unified inbox that lets you see all your email from multiple accounts in one view. You can use gestures to manage your mail, and select multiple conversations to be archived or deleted.

The app supports Gmail, Microsoft Exchange, Outlook, Yahoo Mail, iCloud and IMAP accounts. It also has a passcode feature that lets you keep your email private – this is something that many users will appreciate.

Mailbox – this app aims to get emails out of your inbox as quickly as possible by placing them into categories. For each email, you're encouraged to reply if necessary, delete the message, archive it, or set it aside for later.

You can schedule messages to be returned to your inbox when you're ready to deal with them – this can be in a few hours, days, or a specific date and time. This can be helpful for things like reservations or tickets, so you have the information you need at the appropriate time.

Boxer – if you are looking for an app that hits the middle ground between CloudMagic's power features and Mailbox's ease of use, then Boxer may just be the email app for you. It is gesture-friendly and has very handy quick-reply tools to help you clear your inbox.

Boxer lets you mark email as spam, an option not offered by other email apps. It also integrates with Evernote, Apple's Calendar app, supports Gmail labels and provides a useful to-do list.

Outlook – the official Microsoft Outlook app for tablets, Outlook provides a single unified view of your email, calendar, contacts, and attachments. Swipe to delete, archive, or schedule messages you want to handle later. Easily view your calendar, share available times, and schedule meetings.

Outlook works with Microsoft Exchange, Office 365, Outlook.com, iCloud, Gmail, and Yahoo Mail.

MyMail – MyMail has all of the standard features you'd expect in a modern e-mail app and lets you add existing Gmail, Yahoo!, Outlook, iCloud, AOL, and Hotmail accounts.

A feature of MyMail is that you also get a free My.com account with unlimited storage.

Popular alternatives to the Chrome web browsing app include:

Dolphin – if you want more of a computer browser experience on your iPad, check out Dolphin. Due to its support for gestures and the use of sidebars, the app provides a more intuitive way of browsing the web. It offers many useful options that include a downloads manager, a choice of search engines, tab browsing and much more.

Mercury Browser Pro – Mercury Browser Pro combines the best parts of Safari and Google Chrome into one extremely powerful web browser. Features like ad blocking are built in along with passcode lock, private browsing, social network integration, and gesture support.

The app is capable of syncing bookmarks and data across all your devices with both Firefox and Chrome.

Opera Mini – Opera Mini is considered to be the fastest browser available. To achieve this, it crunches down the size of the websites you visit by compressing images, video and text, making sites lighter and thus faster to load. This does come at a price though, as many of the features found in other browsers have been sacrificed accordingly. However, if speed is what you need, Opera Mini is the one to go for.

Puffin – as with Opera Mini, the feature that really defines Puffin is its speed. This is achieved by compression techniques similar to those used by Opera that reduce website size.

From loading web pages to tabbing through menus, it's smooth and quick. There are also numerous add-ons to choose from, the ability to download files, and much more besides.

Atomic – Atomic is a highly flexible browser that allows the user to set up advanced privacy controls, choose from several color themes, activate an ad-blocker, customize the search engine bar, and view the source of a web page. It also provides Facebook and Twitter integration, and features such as tabs, multi-touch gestures, passcode lock, save page, downloads and more.

Firefox – in terms of performance, i.e. speed at loading pages, Firefox is fairly standard. Where it does shine, however, is in the amount of features it offers. For example, pages can be saved as .PDFs, 'guest' browsing sessions are available, and a handy Reading List lets you save articles for reading later on.

It is also possible to install add-ons that expand the functionality of the browser, with extensions such as Tap Translate, AdBlock Plus, and more.

Finance Apps

Finance apps include calculators, online banking, currency converters, expenditure trackers, stocks and shares monitors, and more. Some of the most popular ones include:

Loan Calculator – Loan Calculator is an easy-to-use financial calculator. It lets you calculate the monthly payment for different types of fixed rate loans such as home mortgage, car, and credit card. Also, you can calculate 'what if' scenarios to determine how additional monthly and yearly payments will help you to pay off your loan earlier and save money paid in interest.

HomeBudget – HomeBudget is an integrated expense tracker designed to help you track your expenses, income, bills, and account balances. It provides support for budgeting, and allows analysis of your expenses and income with charts and graphs.

Calcu Stylish – a very simple, easy-to-use calculator that provides both normal and scientific modes. Features include 12 colorful themes, calculation history, user-defined constants, plus the ability to add and remove functions thus letting you customize the calculator.

Stock Tracker – one of the most comprehensive stock apps, Stock Tracker brings you free streaming live quotes, pre-market/after-hour quotes, portfolio monitoring, advanced full screen charts, push notification based alerts, economic news, event/earnings calendar, market signal scans and much more.

Banking Apps – virtually all the major banks now have apps available. They enable you to check your balance, pay your bills, check on your mortgage, investments, credit cards, and any other financial services you may be using.

Just go to the Play Store, and type your bank's name in the search box.

Property Apps

Virtually all of us investigate the property market from time to time. This can be to buy, rent, or just see what's available and at what price. For the tablet owner, there are a number of apps that make this easy to do right from the comfort of your favorite armchair.

Rightmove – Rightmove is one of the UK's most popular property search engines. With over a million properties featured on Rightmove at any one time, both for sale and to rent, you can use the app's search criteria to pinpoint the exact area you're looking to buy in and specify the features you're looking for.

Just like the online site, the app lets you view floorplans, maps, local information and, of course, pictures. Any properties you save can also be synced to your laptop or computer if you so wish.

Realtor – an American property search engine, Realtor lets you search properties from over 800 multiple listing services – these are refreshed every 15 minutes. Property listing details include property tax and sales history.

Features include being able to draw your own custom search area on the map, and 'Area Scout' that updates search results and values as you move around in the app

UK Property Investing – packed with loads of tips to help you with your property investing in the UK, this app helps you start your journey into the UK property market and is a useful guide when navigating your investment options.

Features include a meeting map to help you find your nearest 'pin' meeting. There is also an event calendar for property training, a forum to swap tips and lots of video advice.

Mortgage Calculator – a simple mortgage calculator that provides optional cost per square foot, and property tax calculations. It will calculate total interest and principal payments over the life of a mortgage. It can tell you if you qualify for a mortgage.

Home Design 3D – with Home Design 3D, designing and changing your home is intuitive and quick. If you want to remodel to create the home of your dreams, the app provides the means of doing so.

With literally thousands of options, including textures, shades, furniture, walls, and much much more, you can create impressive photo-realistic previews of your projects.

Travel & Holiday Apps

A tablet is the ideal device for the traveler who, depending on the destination, means of travel, and reason for travel, will have need of a range of services. Apps are available for literally all these services, some of which we highlight below:

TripAdvisor – thanks to over 150 million reviews and opinions by other travelers, the TripAdvisor app makes it easy to find the lowest airfares, best hotels and restaurants, and most exciting activities, wherever you go.

App features include discovering places near your current location, getting answers to your specific travel questions in the forums plus, of course, adding your own reviews and photos. You can also download maps, reviews, and your saves for over 300 cities worldwide onto your tablet, thus avoiding the need to use expensive data roaming plans while on the move.

Skyscanner – for trips abroad, try Skyscanner. The app lets you search millions of flights from hundreds of airlines around the world – both budget and scheduled – to find the best flights at the cheapest price. When you've found your flight, it links you to the airline or travel agent so you buy directly and get the best deal – all with a few taps.

Features include filters that let you sort results by price, cabin class, airline, and departure times, tab view that lets you easily compare your searches, and chart view that lets you see prices across a week or a month.

Booking.com Hotel – the Booking.com hotel app puts over 612,000 properties at your fingertips. It's not just hotels either – villas, apartments, B & Bs, hostels, and more can be booked in over 212 countries worldwide.

Search results can be filtered by price range, city districts, and facilities such as swimming pools, free Wi-Fi, parking, etc. If you also use Booking. com on your computer, you can sign into your account and have your bookings, recent searches, lists, account details and more automatically synced to the app.

National Rail Inquiries – the must-have app for the UK rail traveler, National Rail Inquiries lets you access detailed, real-time train information direct from your tablet. Innovative technology enables you to track specific trains, find out about disruptions to your journey, and re-plan your journey on the go.

Tripit Travel Organizer – Tripit automatically connects to your email accounts to find travel-confirmation emails, and then turns them into a neat, complete itinerary. Tripit is familiar with purchases you make on all the major search and booking sites, such as Orbitz and Kayak, as well as airlines, car rental services, hotels, restaurant reservations, and more.

Weather Live – Weather Live provides you with current weather conditions and forecasts not just for your current location but multiple locations all around the world.

Features include bad weather warnings and alerts, extended forecasts, cloud, satellite and rain maps, and highly configurable options to name just a few. You can also search for a specific location by zipcode, latitude/longitude, IP, airport code, and name.

XE Currency – an important part of traveling is getting the best conversion rates. XE Currency is an essential app in this regard and offers live proprietary currency rates, charts, and even stores the last updated rates, so it works when an Internet connection isn't available.

You can monitor up to 10 currencies simultaneously, see over 30,000 currency charts for historic rates, calculate prices with the currency converter, and see live proprietary rates that refresh every minute.

GPS Navigation – the GPS Navigation app turns your tablet into a fully functional satellite navigation device. It provides turn-by-turn navigation, speed warnings, street sign displays, 3D-view (isometric) and much more.

The traffic information feature keeps you updated on the current traffic situation – this enables you to avoid being caught up in traffic jams and to make detours round construction sites. It can be used to plan suitable routes whether you are a driver, a pedestrian or a cyclist.

Holiday Checklist – this handy app lets you put together a list of everything you need and ensures you pack it. As you pack, you tick items off the list, and if you attempt to leave with items still unticked, the app will sound an alarm to alert you.

Holiday Checklist comes pre-populated with most items - shirts, t-shirts, dresses, makeup, personal care, gadgets, chargers and so on but you can, of course, add your own items.

Entertainment Apps

Tablets are excellent devices for keeping yourself amused. Apps are available that let you play games, stream movies and TV shows, do crossword puzzles, and much, much more,

Tunein Radio – many people are surprised to find their tablet doesn't come with a radio app. No matter – head over to the Play Store and download Tunein Radio. With it, you can listen to over 100,000 radio stations from around the world, including sports, news, talk and music.

Autodesk SketchBook – Autodesk SketchBook is a professional-grade painting and drawing app. SketchBook offers a number of preset brushes, including pencils, pens and markers.

The app has a slick, smooth interface that's very straightforward and easy to learn. Plus, it continuously auto saves, and has Dropbox integration to ensure you never lose your artwork.

Netflix – Netflix is a UK video streaming service that lets you access thousands of movies and television shows for a small monthly fee. A free one month trial is available. However, it has to be said that much of the content has been around for a while now.

Spotify Music – similar in concept to Netflix, Spotify's forte is music. The app lets you play songs from a library of more than 20 million tracks, build playlists, and get listening recommendations.

Free and premium versions are available. If you decide to pay for a premium account, you get ad-free listening, offline playback, unlimited song skips (instead of the industry-standard six song skips per hour), higher bit-rate streams (320Kbps instead of the standard 128Kbps), and more.

Elevate – rated app of the year, Elevate is a brain training app that lets users train a number of brain faculties, e.g. listening, memory, and comprehension. The app focuses on practical language and math skills such as estimation, comparing values, name recall, as well as reading and listening comprehension.

As with many apps, there are free and premium versions of Elevate, with the premium option providing a better variety of exercises.

CHAPTER 15

Troubleshooting & Maintenance

Tablets are generally very reliable computing devices and are mostly built to high standards. Having said that, things will go wrong with them occasionally, although they will usually be minor issues.

In this chapter, we examine problems typically experienced on tablets and also the measures you can take to keep yours running smoothly.

Troubleshooting Techniques

Major problems with tablets are very rare. Most issues experienced with the devices are little more than temporary glitches that can usually be fixed in one of the following ways:

Reboot the tablet – for the lesser issues that can occur, absolutely the first thing to try is a reboot, i.e. shut the device down and then restart it. This simple action resets internal mechanisms and settings, and will resolve the majority of problems.

To do it, press and hold the Power button until you see the 'Power Off' screen. Tap Power Off to commence the shut-down procedure – when it is complete the screen will be completely black. Then restart the tablet by holding the Power button down until you see the Google logo appear on the screen.

Reset the Tablet – there are hundreds of different settings on your tablet and if any of them become corrupted, a malfunction can occur. Malfunctions with apps can also cause problems. Assuming a reboot hasn't fixed the problem, the next thing to try is to reset the tablet to a time before the problem manifested itself.

To do this, follow the procedure described on page 172 for restoring your tablet from a backup. In step 5, choose a backup created at a time when the tablet was working normally.

Forcibly Close an App – often the problem will not be the tablet itself but rather one of the apps on it. When an app starts misbehaving, simply shut it down and then restart it. This will usually resolve the issue.

To do this, open the Apps screen and then tap Settings. In the Device section, tap Apps. At the top of the screen, tap the 'All' tab (you may need to scroll to the right to see it) to show a list of all apps on the tablet.

To stop one of the apps, tap on it. In the new screen, tap the FORCE STOP button.

Delete and Reinstall an App – in the very unlikely event of an app still misbehaving after being shut down and restarted, your only option is to delete and then reinstall it. To do this, open the Play Store and tap the button at the top-left. On the menu that opens, tap 'My apps' and then tap 'All'.

You will see a number of the apps have an X at the top-right corner. These are the apps that you have downloaded to the tablet and are the only ones that can be deleted. To do so, just tap on the X and then tap OK.

Then tap the back button at the bottom to go back to the Play Store's Home screen, locate the app and reinstall it.

Troubleshooting Ancillary Devices

There is a wide range of ancillary devices that can be connected to a tablet to increase its functionality. These include memory sticks, headsets, adapters of various kinds, battery chargers, speakers, extension keyboards, plus many more.

Inevitably, there will be occasions when one of these devices doesn't work at all, doesn't work properly, or causes the tablet itself to malfunction. As most of the issues likely to occur have already been experienced by someone else and duly documented, it is quite possible that you will find a solution by doing a Google search.

Or, you try the following:

Connections – yes, we know it sounds obvious, but if a device isn't working at all, absolutely the first thing to check is that it is actually connected. If the problem is intermittent, make sure the connection is sound – try wiggling the cable to see if that makes a difference – if it does, there is a loose connection somewhere.

If other devices are part of the circuit, make sure these are switched on and connected. For example, if you cannot access the Internet on your tablet, check the router and its connections.

Power Cycling – a very well known (and effective) troubleshooting technique, you power-cycle a device by switching it off, waiting about 10 seconds, and then switching it back on again.

This action resets the device and it is very effective at resolving spurious problems. If the device in question doesn't have an on/off switch, unplug it from the power source or remove its batteries.

Duff Batteries – if a battery-powered device hasn't been used for a while and doesn't work, open the battery compartment and check the batteries for leakage. If they have leaked, there is quite likely to be a poor or broken connection to the terminals. It goes without saying, of course, that the batteries won't be any good anyway.

Default Settings – the device may provide a number of configuration settings that allow you to set it up. Check you haven't inadvertently caused the problem yourself through an incorrect setting – do this by using the device's 'Restore default settings' option – most have one.

Firmware – many devices have a tiny internal program that tells the device what to do, and thus controls it. This is known as firmware, and firmware updates are almost always available from the manufacturer. Check to see if one is available; if so, download and install it.

Wi-Fi Connection Issues

Wireless networking is brilliant when it works but when it doesn't, it can be a real head-scratcher trying to work out the cause. This is compounded by the fact the problem might not even be anything to do with the tablet!

Working through the following checklist will usually help:

Check That Wi-Fi is Switched On – open the Settings app, and in the 'Wireless & networks' section, tap Wi-Fi. Make sure the on/off switch at the top of the screen is in the On position.

Connection – is your tablet actually connected to a Wi-Fi network? It is not uncommon for network connections to be dropped for no apparent reason. To check, just look at the top-right of your tablet's Status bar. If you see the Wi-Fi icon you are connected.

Range – Wi-Fi works over very short distances, typically between 150 and 300 feet depending on the network hardware. If your tablet is further than this from the source of the network, i.e. the router, it won't be able to get a strong enough signal.

The obvious solution is to move closer to the router. For a permanent fix, you can install a Wi-Fi range extender or booster.

Interference – interference from nearby electrical gadgets can cause flaky and unreliable Wi-Fi connections. Check to see if there are any devices operating in close proximity and either turn them off or move them further away.

Router – Wi-Fi signals are produced by routers. There are three issues that can affect these devices: First, the device may be faulty; second, it's firmware may need updating; third, the device may need replacing with a more recent model.

With regard to the latter, the 802.11ac Wi-Fi standard is currently the fastest and offers a speed of up to 1733 Mbps.

Network Issues – problems can occur with the network your tablet is using. With some networks there is an issue called 'lease time'. Basically, this is the length of time you are allowed to connect to a network with your current dynamic IP address – go over it and your connection is terminated.

All you need to know here is that you can 'renew' the lease time by the simple expedient of turning your Wi-Fi off and then back on. This is not guaranteed to do the trick but almost always does.

Extending Battery Life

Batteries have their pros and cons – they allow devices to be portable but there are cost and inconvenience factors involved. So it is always worth extending the life of your batteries as much as possible.

With regard to tablets, these tips will help considerably:

Screen Brightness – your tablet's screen has a voracious appetite for battery power. Reducing its brightness is just about the most effective way to reduce drain on the battery.

Cycling – rechargeable batteries lose their ability to retain a charge over time. A battery that lasts 10 hours when new, may only last 8 hours a year later. You can delay this inevitable decrease in performance by cycling the battery periodically. Do it by letting the battery go completely flat and then fully recharging it – this should be done every six weeks or so.

Sleep Mode – if you aren't actually using the tablet, put it to sleep by pressing the Power button. Press the same button again to wake the device.

Networks – Wi-Fi makes regular checks for the presence of Wi-Fi networks. Similarly, if your tablet is equipped with cellular networking, it will constantly be on the look-out for cellular signals.

Bluetooth does the same thing – it is continuously checking for nearby Bluetooth devices. All three types of network place a heavy load on the battery, so turn them off whenever possible.

App Updates – by default, the apps on your tablet are kept updated automatically, and the process of constantly checking for, downloading and installing these updates uses battery power.

Give your battery a break by opening the Play Store and swiping across from the left side of the screen. In the menu that slides into view, tap Settings. Then tap 'Auto-update apps' and select 'Do not auto-update apps'. On the same screen, under Notifications, make sure 'Notify when app updates are available' is checked. That way you will know when something needs updating.

Redundant Apps – many apps that are seemingly just sitting there on your tablet doing nothing, are actually working unseen in the background and/or accessing the Internet, and are using battery power while they do it.

After you've been using your tablet for a while, you'll have a good idea which of your tablet's apps are surplus to requirements. While you won't be able to delete the default Google apps, we suggest that any apps you've installed yourself, and don't use, are shown the door as described on page 182.

Managing Storage Space

Currently, tablets are sold with storage capacities of 16, 32, or 64 GB. The latter two are not so bad but if you have a 16 GB model, storage space, or lack of, could well become a problem.

If you intend to store a lot of music, pictures or video on your tablet, it will be as well to keep on top of this issue otherwise, one of these days, you may get a 'running out of storage space' message.

To see how much available storage you have on your tablet:

1. Open the Settings app

2. In the Device section, tap Storage

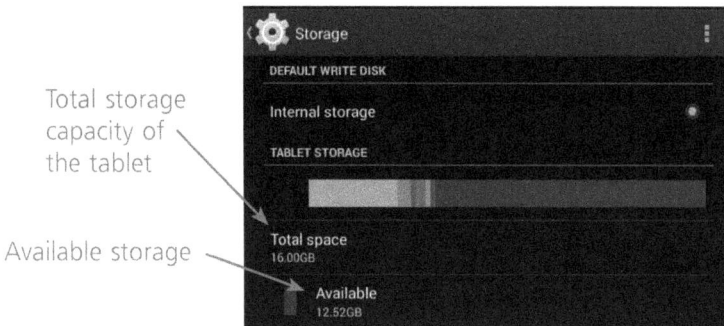

Total storage capacity of the tablet

Available storage

3. On the screen, you will see a graphical representation of how much storage space is available and, below, the total space and available space in figures

Should you ever start running out of space, you have three options:

● Go through your tablet and delete as many apps as you can

● Delete any pictures and video that you can live without – these, and music to a lesser extent, use up more storage space than anything else

● Open the Storage screen as above and tap 'Cached data'. On a well used tablet, this can contain a large amount of unneeded data. In the 'Clear cached data?' window, tap OK to empty the cache

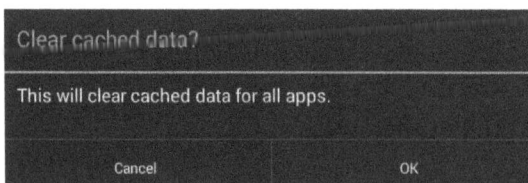

Index

T

U